Betty Crocker

Smoothies

Plus Bonus Juicing Section!

HOUGHTON MIFFLIN HARCOURT
Boston • New York • 2015

GENERAL MILLS

Creative Content and Publishing Director: Elizabeth Nientimp

Food Content Marketing Manager: Heather Reid Liebo

Senior Editor: Grace Wells

Editor: Catherine Swanson

Kitchen Manager: Ann Stuart

Recipe Development and Testing: Betty Crocker Kitchens

Photography: General Mills Photography Studios and Image Library

HOUGHTON MIFFLIN HARCOURT

Publisher: Natalie Chapman

Editorial Director: Cindy Kitchel

Executive Editor: Anne Ficklen

Editorial Associate: Molly Aronica

Managing Editor: Marina Padakis

Production Editor: Helen Seachrist

Cover Design: Tai Blanche

Interior Design and Layout: Tai Blanche

Production Coordinator: Kimberly Kiefer

Published by Houghton Mifflin Harcourt

For information about permission to reproduce selections from this book, write to Permissions, Houghton Mifflin Harcourt Publishing Company, 215 Park Avenue South, New York, New York 10003.

www.hmhco.com

Library of Congress Cataloging-in-Publication Data

Crocker, Betty.
 Betty Crocker smoothies.
   pages cm
 Includes index.
 ISBN 978-0-544-45434-7 (trade paper) ; 978-0-544-45362-3 (ebk.)
 1. Smoothies (Beverages) 2. Blenders (Cooking) I. Title. II. Title: Smoothies.
 TX840.B5C755 2014
 641.8'75—dc23
 2014021637

Manufactured in the United States of America

DOC 10 9 8 7 6 5 4 3 2 1

Cover photos: Watermelon-Kiwi-Banana Smoothies (page 70), Nutritious Green Smoothies (page 86), Raspberry Lemonade Pops (page 188), Purple Juice Pick-Me-Up (page 212)

The Betty Crocker Kitchens seal guarantees success in your kitchen. Every recipe has been tested in America's Most Trusted Kitchens™ to meet our high standards of reliability, easy preparation and great taste.

FIND MORE GREAT IDEAS AT
BettyCrocker.com

Dear Friends,

Who doesn't love smoothies? Whether it's a quick meal on the go or a thirst-quenching snack, smoothies are loved by all ages. They are a snap to make in endless flavor combinations and are an easy way to add fruits or vegetables to your day. Make any of these recipes next time you want a tasty sipper, have a lot of fruit begging to be used or even as inspiration for making your own tasty concoctions!

In this book of Betty Crocker *Smoothies,* there is a full menu of delicious recipes to choose from. Are you looking for something kids will drink? You'll want to try Berry Blast Smoothies, page 28. Or, for a protein smoothie on the way to work, sip on Tea-Berry Smash, page 38. And if you simply want to increase the amount of vegetables you are eating in a day, we have a whole chapter of smoothies that contain vegetables. Plus, there are even dairy-free options and calorie-controlled smoothies—each with 150 calories or less—look for the icons to find them easily.

But don't think we stopped at smoothies in glasses, because these delicious drinks go beyond sipping. Be sure to check out a whole chapter loaded with smoothies that come in different forms—pops, cubes and poppers. Can you say, "yum"?

Also, be sure to browse the special bonus section dedicated to juicing. Whether you're a beginning juicer or a pro, you'll love the helpful juicing information and recipes for making beautiful, delicious juices at home.

So grab a glass and your blender, and let's get started. Let's make smoothies!

Sincerely,

Betty Crocker

contents

build the best smoothies

Making smoothies is a cinch—but making great smoothies takes just a few building blocks. In this section, you'll find everything you need to know to whip up wonderfully tasty smoothies.

start with a base

Pick one of these bases and place it in the blender before other ingredients so it will be easier to blend everything smoothly:

- Yogurt (any variety will work and Greek yogurt will be a little thicker)
- Soymilk, almond milk or coconut milk
- Coconut water or sparkling water (plain or flavored)
- Tea (any variety will work but it should be cooled)
- Juice
- Milk (can be used as long as citrus fruit isn't in the smoothies, or the milk could curdle)
- Ice cream, frozen yogurt or gelato

use ripe fruit

If the fruit is good to eat, go ahead and use it. If it isn't ripe yet, or if it's overly ripe and past the point of tasting good, then it won't make good-tasting smoothies. You can buy many types of fresh fruit to cut up and freeze in small resealable food storage plastic bags. But it's also easy to buy already cut-up frozen fruit and keep it on hand in your freezer. Canned fruit can also be used. Use just one fruit, or mix and match several—the possible combinations are endless, so use your imagination and be creative!

resist adding water

Adding ice cubes to make your smoothies colder or water to make the mixture thinner can dilute the flavor, unless this is part of the recipe. Instead, start with fresh, cold or frozen fruit to make your smoothies super-cold without the need for ice. Or, use ice cubes made from juice or blended fruit (see our Fruit Smoothie Cubes recipe, page 200).

add smoothie boosters

Adding special ingredients can give the same-old smoothies new life or take your recipe in a different flavor direction. Added ingredients can also bump up the nutritional benefits of your smoothies, making them even more beneficial to sip. Be sure to check out the smoothie boosters, page 8.

lift the flavor

Many of the smoothie boosters (page 8) can be used to add flavor to your smoothies. Or try adding a little vanilla to perk up the flavor or enhance the fruit flavors in your smoothies. Instead of plain or vanilla yogurt, try adding a flavored yogurt instead. For example, lime yogurt can add just a hint of lime to berry smoothies. Experiment by adding just a little bit at a time. You can always add more.

tweak the sweetness

Taste your smoothies before adding any additional sweeteners. The ripe fruit often provides all the sweetness you'll need. If it isn't as sweet as you would like it, you could add banana, honey, agave nectar or a little granulated or powdered sugar. Start with a small amount; blend and add more if needed.

smoothie boosters

Smoothies can be a great way to add some healthful fruits and vegetables to your diet. With the addition of a variety of ingredients, you can quickly and easily bump up the nutritional makeup of your homemade smoothies and add more flavor too. Experiment by adding one or more of the following delicious choices to your smoothies. Start by adding in small amounts, then taste and see what you think. You can always add more.

everyday additions

Here are some suggestions for adding flavor and texture to smoothies. You might have some of them on hand but they are all easy to find at the supermarket.

- **Leftover cooked grains:** If you have some leftover cooked brown rice, quinoa or oats in your refrigerator, go ahead and add a tablespoon or two to smoothies for a bit of additional fiber and whole-grain goodness. Uncooked rolled oats can also be added but will absorb liquid, so it may be necessary to add a bit of extra liquid.

- **Cottage cheese:** Nonfat cottage cheese can add body, creaminess and protein to smoothies without a big hit in calories. Blended up with other ingredients, it adds nice texture but very little flavor.

- **Spinach or kale:** Blend in some fresh spinach or kale leaves for an added dose of vitamins and fiber. Start with just a few leaves and add more as you like.

- **Green tea:** Use brewed cool green tea as all or part of the liquid in smoothies to add some flavor.

- **Peanut butter or other nut butters:** A good source of protein and monounsaturated fats, nut butters also add flavor to smoothies. Reduced-fat peanut butters can be loaded with sugar and other additives, so look for natural peanut butter or other nut butters, which are typically made with just nuts or nuts and salt. To help nut butter mix well in smoothies, spread it on a piece of fruit before adding to the blender.

- **Pomegranate juice:** Pomegranate juice has wonderful flavor and has been touted for its health value. Be sure to look for pure pomegranate juice and not juice cocktails, which can contain large amounts of sugar.

- **Silken tofu:** This tasty food bumps up the protein of smoothies, thickens slightly and adds mild flavor too.

nature's additions

Adding a bit of extra fiber or nutrients is doable with these ingredients. Look for these items at health food stores. Purchase in small amounts to see if you enjoy the flavor and texture they add, then purchase more as you learn what you like best.

- **Flaxseed:** It's easiest to purchase ground flaxseed if it is available. Store the flaxseed in the refrigerator or freezer to keep it fresh.

- **Chia seeds:** Blended into smoothies, chia seed provides bulk and many nutrients.

- **Hemp seeds:** This is a plant-based source of protein that adds a variety of healthful nutrients.

- **Raw pumpkin seeds:** These tasty seeds add flavor and some nutrients to smoothies.

- **Coconut water:** This is the clear liquid from young, green coconuts, and it has a sweet, nutty flavor. Use it as part or all of the liquid in smoothies.

- **Matcha:** These are simply green tea leaves that have been ground. Matcha provides ingredients in concentrated form since the entire leaf is consumed. Use it in small quantities because the flavor can overpower the flavor of smoothies.

- **Vanilla kefir:** This drinkable yogurt has calcium and other nutrients, making it a nice addition to smoothies.

- **Protein powder:** This powder adds protein but not a lot of extra flavor to smoothies. Add it in small amounts to start.

Fruit Smoothies

greek mixed berry smoothies

PREP TIME: 5 Minutes • **START TO FINISH:** 5 Minutes • 2 servings

¾ cup fat-free (skim) milk

1 container (5.3 oz) mixed berry Greek yogurt

½ cup Nature Valley™ oats 'n honey protein granola (from 11-oz bag)

1 pouch (4.5 oz) mixed berry frozen smoothie

1 In blender, place all ingredients. Cover; blend on high speed 1 minute to 1 minute 30 seconds, stopping to scrape sides as necessary, until smooth.

2 Pour into 2 glasses. Serve immediately.

1 Serving: Calories 220; Total Fat 4g (Saturated Fat 0g; Trans Fat 0g); Cholesterol 0mg; Sodium 160mg; Total Carbohydrate 35g (Dietary Fiber 2g); Protein 12g **Exchanges:** ½ Starch, 1 Fruit, 1 Other Carbohydrate, ½ Skim Milk **Carbohydrate Choices:** 2

boost it

To easily crush the granola bars, use a rolling pin to crush them before unwrapping.

mix it up

Lemon, vanilla or plain yogurt can be used instead of the mixed berry yogurt.

triple berry–banana smoothies

PREP TIME: 10 Minutes • **START TO FINISH:** 10 Minutes • 2 servings (1¼ cups each)

¾ cup frozen harvest berries (strawberries, blackberries and blueberries), from 10-oz bag

½ banana, sliced (1 cup)

½ cup low-fat soymilk or fat-free (skim) milk

1 container (6 oz) vanilla yogurt

1 In blender, place all ingredients. Cover; blend on high speed about 1 minute or until smooth.

2 Pour into 2 glasses. Serve immediately.

1 Serving: Calories 160; Total Fat 2g (Saturated Fat 1g; Trans Fat 0g); Cholesterol 0mg; Sodium 100mg; Total Carbohydrate 27g (Dietary Fiber 3g); Protein 7g **Exchanges:** ½ Starch, 1 Fruit, ½ Skim Milk **Carbohydrate Choices:** 2

mix it up

For well-blended smoothies, stop the blender halfway through blending and uncover; scrape down the sides of the container and continue blending.

Garnish the smoothies with additional berries, frozen or fresh.

raspberry-banana-yogurt smoothies

PREP TIME: 5 Minutes • **START TO FINISH:** 5 Minutes • 2 servings (about 1½ cups each)

1 container (6 oz) French vanilla low-fat yogurt

1½ cups soymilk

1 cup unsweetened frozen or fresh raspberries

1 medium banana, sliced (1 cup)

1 In blender or food processor, place all ingredients. Cover; blend on high speed about 30 seconds or until smooth.

2 Pour into 2 glasses. Serve immediately.

1 Serving: Calories 290; Total Fat 4g (Saturated Fat 1g; Trans Fat 0g); Cholesterol 5mg; Sodium 160mg; Total Carbohydrate 54g (Dietary Fiber 10g); Protein 9g **Exchanges:** 1 Fruit, 2 Other Carbohydrate, 1 Low-Fat Milk **Carbohydrate Choices:** 3½

mix it up

If serving with straws, purchase larger diameter straws to accommodate the thicker texture of these smoothies.

granola-berry-banana smoothies

PREP TIME: 5 Minutes • **START TO FINISH:** 5 Minutes • 2 servings

2 containers (6 oz each) strawberry or red raspberry low-fat or fat-free yogurt

½ cup milk

½ cup fresh strawberry halves or raspberries

1 medium banana, sliced (1 cup)

2 pouches (1.5 oz each) oats 'n honey crunchy granola bars (4 bars)

1 In blender, place yogurt, milk, strawberry halves and banana slices. Break up 3 granola bars; add to blender. Cover; blend on high speed 10 seconds. Scrape down sides of blender. Cover; blend about 20 seconds longer or until smooth.

2 Pour into 2 glasses. Crumble remaining granola bar; sprinkle over smoothie mixture in each glass. Serve immediately.

1 Serving: Calories 450; Total Fat 9g (Saturated Fat 2.5g; Trans Fat 0g); Cholesterol 15mg; Sodium 270mg; Total Carbohydrate 81g (Dietary Fiber 4g); Protein 12g **Exchanges:** 4 Starch, ½ Fruit, 1 Other Carbohydrate, 1 Fat **Carbohydrate Choices:** 5½

mix it up

Top each smoothie with fresh strawberries or raspberries.

Fresh pineapple can be substituted for the strawberries or raspberries for a different flavor combination that is delicious.

berry-banana smoothies

PREP TIME: 10 Minutes • **START TO FINISH:** 10 Minutes • 2 servings (about 1 cup each)

1 cup vanilla, plain, strawberry or raspberry low-fat yogurt (from two 6-oz containers)

½ cup Cheerios™ cereal

2 tablespoons ground flaxseed or flaxseed meal

½ cup fresh strawberry halves or raspberries, or frozen whole strawberries

½ cup fat-free (skim) milk

1 to 2 tablespoons sugar

½ banana, sliced (1 cup)

1 In blender, place all ingredients. Cover; blend on high speed 10 seconds. Scrape down sides of blender. Cover; blend about 20 seconds longer or until smooth.

2 Pour into 2 glasses. Serve immediately.

1 Serving: Calories 270; Total Fat 3.5g (Saturated Fat 0.5g; Trans Fat 0g); Cholesterol 0mg; Sodium 170mg; Total Carbohydrate 50g (Dietary Fiber 4g); Protein 10g   **Exchanges:** 2 Fruit, 1 Skim Milk, 1 Fat   **Carbohydrate Choices:** 3

boost it

Yogurt and fortified cereal team up to make this a smoothie that will give you an extra energy boost any time of day!

mix it up

Make berry-kiwifruit smoothies by substituting 2 peeled kiwifruit for the ½ banana.

strawberry-banana-nut-oatmeal smoothies

PREP TIME: 5 Minutes • **START TO FINISH:** 5 Minutes • 2 servings

1 cup fat-free (skim) milk

1 packet regular-flavor instant oatmeal

¼ cup walnuts

1 pouch (7.6 oz) strawberry-banana-flavor pieces of frozen fruit and yogurt chips smoothie mix

1 In blender, place all ingredients. Cover; blend on high speed 1 minute to 1 minute 30 seconds, stopping to scrape down sides as necessary, until smooth.

2 Pour into 2 glasses. Serve immediately.

1 Serving: Calories 270; Total Fat 12g (Saturated Fat 1g; Trans Fat 0g); Cholesterol 0mg; Sodium 120mg; Total Carbohydrate 32g (Dietary Fiber 3g); Protein 9g   **Exchanges:** ½ Starch, 1 Other Carbohydrate, 1 Skim Milk, 2 Fat   **Carbohydrate Choices:** 2

mix it up

Substitute strawberries and cream or bananas and cream instant oatmeal for the regular.

Look for the smoothie mix in the freezer section of your grocery store, usually near the frozen fruit.

blue-banana protein smoothie shake

PREP TIME: 10 Minutes • **START TO FINISH:** 10 Minutes • 1 serving (1¾ cups)

½ cup frozen chopped banana

½ cup frozen blueberries

¾ cup milk

1 scoop vanilla protein powder (6 tablespoons)

1 In blender, place all ingredients. Cover; blend on high speed until smooth.

2 Pour into large glass. Serve immediately.

1 Serving: Calories 340; Total Fat 4.5g (Saturated Fat 2g; Trans Fat 0g); Cholesterol 10mg; Sodium 180mg; Total Carbohydrate 44g (Dietary Fiber 5g); Protein 31g **Exchanges:** ½ Starch, 1 Fruit, ½ Other Carbohydrate, ½ Skim Milk, ½ Low-Fat Milk, 3 Very Lean Meat **Carbohydrate Choices:** 3

mix it up

Use whatever berries you have on hand or that are on sale at your supermarket, such as raspberries or strawberries.

If you'd like to make smoothies for two, simply double the ingredients.

berry-peach smoothies

PREP TIME: 5 Minutes • **START TO FINISH:** 5 Minutes • 4 servings (about 1 cup each)

1 cup frozen whole raspberries without syrup

¾ cup milk

2 tablespoons sugar-free low-calorie peach instant iced tea mix

1 container (6 oz) white chocolate–raspberry low-fat yogurt

1 bag (16 oz) frozen sliced peaches without syrup, 4 slices reserved and thawed

Additional frozen (thawed) raspberries without syrup for garnish, if desired

1 In blender, place raspberries, milk, tea mix and yogurt. Cover; blend on high speed 10 to 20 seconds or until smooth. Add half of the peach slices; cover and blend on high speed until smooth. Add remaining peaches; cover and blend until smooth.

2 Pour into 4 glasses. Garnish each with peach slice and raspberries. Serve immediately.

1 Serving: Calories 140; Total Fat 2g (Saturated Fat 1g; Trans Fat 0g); Cholesterol 5mg; Sodium 45mg; Total Carbohydrate 26g (Dietary Fiber 5g); Protein 4g   **Exchanges:** 1 Starch, 1 Fruit   **Carbohydrate Choices:** 2

berry blast smoothies

PREP TIME: 10 Minutes • **START TO FINISH:** 10 Minutes • 2 servings (1 cup each)

1   cup frozen blueberries

¾   cup chopped peeled apple

⅓   cup fat-free (skim) milk

1   container (6 oz) vanilla
     fat-free yogurt

1   tablespoon real maple
     syrup or honey

1 In blender, place all ingredients. Cover; blend on high speed about 1 minute or until smooth.

2 Pour into 2 glasses. Serve immediately.

1 Serving: Calories 200; Total Fat 2g (Saturated Fat 1g; Trans Fat 0g); Cholesterol 5mg; Sodium 75mg; Total Carbohydrate 40g (Dietary Fiber 3g); Protein 6g   **Exchanges:** ½ Starch, ½ Fruit, 1½ Other Carbohydrate, ½ Skim Milk   **Carbohydrate Choices:** 2½

mix it up

Braeburn, Cortland or Delicious apples would taste great in these smoothies.

Greek yogurt is a nice substitute for the fat-free yogurt in the recipe and will make your smoothies a little thicker.

berry smoothies

PREP TIME: 5 Minutes • **START TO FINISH:** 5 Minutes • 2 servings

1 cup frozen unsweetened
blueberries or raspberries

1¼ cups vanilla soymilk

1 container (6 oz) French
vanilla low-fat yogurt

Honey, if desired

1 In blender or food processor, place blueberries, soymilk and yogurt. Cover; blend on high speed about 1 minute or until smooth. Sweeten to taste with honey.

2 Pour into 2 glasses. Serve immediately.

1 Serving: Calories 210; Total Fat 3.5g (Saturated Fat 1g; Trans Fat 0g); Cholesterol 5mg; Sodium 150mg; Total Carbohydrate 37g (Dietary Fiber 3g); Protein 6g **Exchanges:** ½ Fruit, 1 Other Carbohydrate, 1 Skim Milk, ½ Fat **Carbohydrate Choices:** 2½

mix it up
Chill glasses in advance to keep this drink cold longer on a warm day.

strawberry-bran smoothies

PREP TIME: 5 Minutes • **START TO FINISH:** 5 Minutes • 2 servings (1 cup each)

1 container (6 oz) strawberry low-fat yogurt

1 cup fresh strawberry halves or frozen unsweetened whole strawberries

¾ cup fat-free (skim) milk

2 tablespoons Fiber One™ original bran cereal

1 In blender, place all ingredients. Cover; blend on high speed 10 seconds. Scrape down sides of blender. Cover; blend about 20 seconds longer or until smooth.

2 Pour into 2 glasses. Serve immediately.

1 Serving: Calories 160; Total Fat 1g (Saturated Fat 0.5g; Trans Fat 0g); Cholesterol 5mg; Sodium 90mg; Total Carbohydrate 30g (Dietary Fiber 3g); Protein 6g **Exchanges:** ½ Starch, ½ Fruit, ½ Other Carbohydrate, ½ Skim Milk **Carbohydrate Choices:** 2

boost it

For a smoother consistency, crush the cereal in a small resealable food-storage plastic bag with a rolling pin before adding it to the ingredients in the blender.

strawberry-cranberry smoothies

PREP TIME: 10 Minutes • **START TO FINISH:** 10 Minutes • 2 servings (1¼ cups each)

1¼ cups frozen unsweetened whole strawberries

1 small apple, peeled, cut into chunks

½ cup cranberry juice cocktail

1 container (6 oz) vanilla low-fat yogurt

1 In blender, place all ingredients. Cover; blend on high speed about 30 seconds or until smooth.

2 Pour into 2 glasses. Serve immediately.

1 Serving: Calories 200; Total Fat 1.5g (Saturated Fat 0.5g; Trans Fat 0g); Cholesterol 0mg; Sodium 60mg; Total Carbohydrate 41g (Dietary Fiber 4g); Protein 5g **Exchanges:** 1 Fruit, 1½ Other Carbohydrate, ½ Skim Milk **Carbohydrate Choices:** 3

mix it up

For extra-chilled smoothies, place the glasses in the freezer at least 15 minutes before blending the fruit mixture.

If you don't have cranberry juice cocktail, orange juice would make a great-tasting substitution.

strawberry–key lime smoothies

PREP TIME: 10 Minutes • **START TO FINISH:** 10 Minutes • 2 servings

1 cup frozen unsweetened whole strawberries

½ cup calcium-enriched orange juice or fat-free (skim) milk

2 containers (6 oz each) Key lime pie fat-free yogurt

1 In blender, place all ingredients. Cover; blend on high speed about 1 minute or until smooth.

2 Pour into 2 glasses. Serve immediately.

1 Serving: Calories 160; Total Fat 0g (Saturated Fat 0g; Trans Fat 0g); Cholesterol 0mg; Sodium 85mg; Total Carbohydrate 33g (Dietary Fiber 2g); Protein 6g **Exchanges:** ½ Starch, 1 Fruit, ½ Other Carbohydrate, ½ Skim Milk **Carbohydrate Choices:** 2

tea-berry smash

PREP TIME: 5 Minutes • **START TO FINISH:** 5 Minutes • 2 servings (1½ cups each)

1 cup brewed cold green tea

1 scoop (⅓ cup) whey protein powder

1 teaspoon honey

1 pouch (7.6 oz) blueberry-pomegranate-flavor pieces of frozen fruit and yogurt chips smoothie mix

1 In blender, place all ingredients. Cover; blend on high speed 1 minute to 1 minute 30 seconds, stopping blender to scrape down sides as necessary, until smooth.

2 Pour into 2 glasses. Serve immediately.

1 Serving: Calories 140; Total Fat 1.5g (Saturated Fat 0g; Trans Fat 0g); Cholesterol 0mg; Sodium 55mg; Total Carbohydrate 19g (Dietary Fiber 2g); Protein 11g **Exchanges:** ½ Starch, 1 Other Carbohydrate, 1½ Very Lean Meat **Carbohydrate Choices:** 1

mix it up

If you like sweeter smoothies, add another teaspoon of honey to the blender mixture.

apple-berry smoothies

PREP TIME: 5 Minutes • **START TO FINISH:** 5 Minutes • 2 servings

1 cup fat-free (skim) milk

1 unpeeled Granny Smith apple, cored, coarsely chopped

1 pouch (7.6 oz) triple berry–flavor pieces of frozen fruit and yogurt chips smoothie mix

1 In blender, place all ingredients. Cover; blend on high speed 1 minute to 1 minute 30 seconds, stopping blender to scrape down sides as necessary, until smooth.

2 Pour into 2 glasses. Serve immediately.

1 Serving: Calories 170; Total Fat 2g (Saturated Fat 0g; Trans Fat 0g); Cholesterol 0mg; Sodium 80mg; Total Carbohydrate 33g (Dietary Fiber 4g); Protein 6g **Exchanges:** ½ Starch, 1 Fruit, ½ Other Carbohydrate, ½ Skim Milk **Carbohydrate Choices:** 2

mix it up

Any apple will work, but sweeter varieties will add additional sweetness to the smoothies. Or ½ cup applesauce can be used in place of the fresh apple.

blueberry-orange smoothies

PREP TIME: 5 Minutes • **START TO FINISH: 5 Minutes** • **2 servings (1 cup each)**

1 cup frozen blueberries

½ cup orange juice

1 teaspoon grated orange peel

1 container (6 oz) blueberry Greek yogurt

1 In blender, place all ingredients. Cover; blend on high speed about 1 minute or until smooth.

2 Pour into 2 glasses. Serve immediately.

1 Serving: Calories 140; Total Fat 0g (Saturated Fat 0g; Trans Fat 0g); Cholesterol 5mg; Sodium 50mg; Total Carbohydrate 27g (Dietary Fiber 2g); Protein 7g **Exchanges:** 1½ Fruit, ½ Skim Milk **Carbohydrate Choices:** 2

boost it

For an additional boost of calcium, use calcium-fortified orange juice.

mix it up

Surprise your family with a smoothie breakfast! Serve smoothies with toasted bagels topped with reduced-fat cream cheese for a delicious change from cereal and juice.

berry-orange blasters

PREP TIME: 5 Minutes • **START TO FINISH:** 5 Minutes • 2 servings (1 cup each)

1 cup calcium-enriched orange juice

4 teaspoons honey

1 pouch (7.6 oz) strawberry-banana-flavor pieces of frozen fruit and yogurt chips smoothie mix

1 In blender, place all ingredients. Cover; blend on high speed 1 minute to 1 minute 30 seconds, stopping blender to scrape down sides as necessary, until smooth.

2 Pour into 2 glasses. Serve immediately.

1 Serving: Calories 180; Total Fat 1g (Saturated Fat 0g; Trans Fat 0g); Cholesterol 0mg; Sodium 35mg; Total Carbohydrate 39g (Dietary Fiber 1g); Protein 2g **Exchanges:** 1 Starch, ½ Fruit, 1 Other Carbohydrate **Carbohydrate Choices:** 2½

mix it up

If these smoothies are too tart for you, add another teaspoon of honey.

strawberry-orange smoothies

PREP TIME: 5 Minutes • **START TO FINISH:** 5 Minutes • 2 servings

1½ cups vanilla soymilk

1 bag (10 oz) frozen strawberries, partially thawed

1 medium banana, cut into chunks

⅓ cup calcium-enriched orange juice

Honey, if desired

1 In blender or food processor, place soymilk, strawberries, banana and orange juice. Cover; blend on high speed about 1 minute or until smooth. Sweeten to taste with honey.

2 Pour into 2 glasses. Serve immediately.

1 Serving: Calories 210; Total Fat 3g (Saturated Fat 0g; Trans Fat 0g); Cholesterol 0mg; Sodium 90mg; Total Carbohydrate 40g (Dietary Fiber 5g); Protein 6g **Exchanges:** ½ Starch, 1 Fruit, 1 Other Carbohydrate, ½ Skim Milk, ½ Fat **Carbohydrate Choices:** 2½

mix it up

If you are serving more than two people, have all of your ingredients ready. Then, just blend everything a second time.

creamy raspberry-pear smoothies

PREP TIME: 10 Minutes • **START TO FINISH:** 10 Minutes • 2 servings (1¼ cups each)

1¼ cups frozen raspberries

1 small pear, peeled, cut into chunks

⅔ cup fat-free (skim) milk

1 container (6 oz) vanilla low-fat yogurt

1 In blender, place all ingredients. Cover; blend on high speed about 30 seconds or until smooth.

2 Pour into 2 glasses. Serve immediately.

1 Serving: Calories 240; Total Fat 2g (Saturated Fat 1g; Trans Fat 0g); Cholesterol 5mg; Sodium 95mg; Total Carbohydrate 46g (Dietary Fiber 12g); Protein 9g **Exchanges:** 1 Starch, 1 Fruit, ½ Other Carbohydrate, ½ Skim Milk **Carbohydrate Choices:** 3

mix it up

Garnish these smoothies with a few thawed raspberries and sliced pears.

For extra-frosty smoothies, chill your glasses in the freezer for at least 15 minutes before making the smoothies.

raspberry lemonade smoothies

PREP TIME: 10 Minutes • **START TO FINISH:** 10 Minutes • 4 servings (1 cup each)

1 cup refrigerated raspberry lemonade (from 64-oz container)

2 ripe bananas, thickly sliced

1½ cups fresh raspberries

2 containers (6 oz each) red raspberry low-fat yogurt

1 In blender or food processor, place all ingredients. Cover; blend on high speed about 1 minute or until smooth and creamy.

2 Pour into 4 glasses. Serve immediately.

1 Serving: Calories 180; Total Fat 1.5g (Saturated Fat 0.5g; Trans Fat 0g); Cholesterol 0mg; Sodium 50mg; Total Carbohydrate 42g (Dietary Fiber 5g); Protein 5g **Exchanges:** 1 Fruit, 1½ Other Carbohydrate, ½ Skim Milk **Carbohydrate Choices:** 2½

mix it up

If you don't have the fresh raspberries, go ahead and use frozen raspberries that are slightly thawed instead. Float a few fresh raspberries on top of each smoothie if you like.

fresh blackberry smoothie

PREP TIME: 10 Minutes • **START TO FINISH:** 10 Minutes • 1 serving

1 container (6 oz) blackberry fat-free yogurt

½ cup fresh or frozen blackberries

½ cup orange juice

Additional blackberries and fresh mint, if desired

1 In blender, place yogurt, ½ cup blackberries and the orange juice. Cover; blend on medium speed about 2 minutes or until smooth.

2 Pour into glass. Garnish with additional blackberries and fresh mint. Serve immediately.

1 Serving: Calories 200; Total Fat 0.5g (Saturated Fat 0g; Trans Fat 0g); Cholesterol 0mg; Sodium 75mg; Total Carbohydrate 41g (Dietary Fiber 4g); Protein 7g **Exchanges:** 1 Fruit, 1½ Other Carbohydrate, 1 Very Lean Meat **Carbohydrate Choices:** 3

frosty blueberry-peach smoothies

PREP TIME: 10 Minutes • **START TO FINISH:** 10 Minutes • 2 servings (1⅓ cups each)

1 cup frozen sliced peaches
(from 10-oz bag)

¾ cup frozen blueberries

⅔ cup fat-free (skim) milk

1 container (6 oz) peach
low-fat yogurt

Additional frozen sliced
peaches, thawed, if desired

1 In blender, place 1 cup peaches, blueberries, milk and yogurt. Cover; blend on high speed about 1 minute or until smooth.

2 Pour into 2 glasses. Garnish with additional peach slices. Serve immediately.

1 Serving: Calories 200; Total Fat 1.5g (Saturated Fat 0.5g; Trans Fat 0g); Cholesterol 5mg; Sodium 90mg; Total Carbohydrate 38g (Dietary Fiber 4g); Protein 7g **Exchanges:** ½ Starch, 1 Fruit, ½ Other Carbohydrate, ½ Skim Milk **Carbohydrate Choices:** 2½

mix it up

If you don't have peach yogurt, you can use vanilla yogurt instead.

mango-berry smoothies

PREP TIME: 5 Minutes • **START TO FINISH:** 5 Minutes • 3 servings (1 cup each)

1 container (6 oz) strawberry low-fat yogurt

1¼ cups vanilla or original soymilk

1 cup cubed ripe mango

1 cup frozen raspberries or strawberries

1 In blender, place all ingredients. Cover; blend on high speed about 1 minute or until smooth.

2 Pour into 3 glasses. Serve immediately.

1 Serving: Calories 180; Total Fat 2.5g (Saturated Fat 0.5g; Trans Fat 0g); Cholesterol 0mg; Sodium 95mg; Total Carbohydrate 33g (Dietary Fiber 6g); Protein 5g **Exchanges:** 1 Fruit, 1 Other Carbohydrate, ½ Low-Fat Milk **Carbohydrate Choices:** 2

berries and mango smoothie

PREP TIME: 10 Minutes • **START TO FINISH:** 10 Minutes • 1 serving

½ cup cubed ripe mango

½ cup fresh or frozen raspberries

½ cup halved fresh or frozen strawberries

½ cup orange juice

1 tablespoon honey

1 In blender, place all ingredients. Cover; blend on medium speed about 2 minutes or until smooth.

2 Pour into glass. If desired, garnish with an additional mango slice, raspberry and strawberry. Serve immediately.

1 Serving: Calories 250; Total Fat 1g (Saturated Fat 0g; Trans Fat 0g); Cholesterol 0mg; Sodium 5mg; Total Carbohydrate 57g (Dietary Fiber 7g); Protein 3g **Exchanges:** 1 Starch, 2 Fruit, 1 Other Carbohydrate **Carbohydrate Choices:** 4

blueberry-mango smoothie: Substitute 1 cup fresh or frozen blueberries for the strawberries and raspberries.

mix it up

Double the ingredients if you would like to make this a recipe for two.

creamy peach smoothies

PREP TIME: 10 Minutes • **START TO FINISH:** 10 Minutes • 3 servings

1   cup frozen sliced peaches
    (from 10-oz bag)

1   banana, thickly sliced

1½ cups orange juice

1   tablespoon honey

1   container (6 oz) French
    vanilla low-fat yogurt

1 In blender or food processor, place peaches, banana, orange juice and honey. Cover; blend on high speed about 1 minute or until smooth and creamy.

2 Pour about ¼ cup mixture into each of 3 glasses; add 1 tablespoon yogurt to each. Repeat layers 2 more times. Swirl yogurt into peach mixture with knife. Serve immediately.

1 Serving: Calories 200; Total Fat 1g (Saturated Fat 0g; Trans Fat 0g); Cholesterol 0mg; Sodium 35mg; Total Carbohydrate 44g (Dietary Fiber 2g); Protein 3g **Exchanges:** 1 Starch, 2 Fruit **Carbohydrate Choices:** 3

mix it up

Instead of swirling the yogurt into the drink, you can add the yogurt to the other ingredients in the blender and blend everything together.

peachy pineapple smoothies

PREP TIME: 5 Minutes • **START TO FINISH:** 5 Minutes • 3 servings (1 cup each)

1 container (6 oz) French vanilla low-fat yogurt

1 cup peach or mango chunks

1¼ cups soymilk

¼ cup pineapple juice

1 In blender or food processor, place all ingredients. Cover; blend on high speed about 1 minute or until smooth.

2 Pour into 3 glasses. Garnish as desired. Serve immediately.

1 Serving: Calories 120; Total Fat 2g (Saturated Fat 0.5g; Trans Fat 0g); Cholesterol 0mg; Sodium 95mg; Total Carbohydrate 22g (Dietary Fiber 0g); Protein 4g **Exchanges:** 1 Other Carbohydrate, ½ Low-Fat Milk **Carbohydrate Choices:** 1½

peachy white tea smoothies

PREP TIME: 5 Minutes • **START TO FINISH:** 30 Minutes • 2 servings (1¼ cups each)

2 cups soymilk

8 bags peach-flavor white tea

3 cups frozen sliced peaches

¼ cup honey

1 In 1-quart saucepan, heat soymilk just to boiling over medium-high heat, stirring constantly; remove from heat. Add tea bags and push into soymilk; let stand 5 minutes. Remove and discard tea bags. Place saucepan with soymilk mixture in freezer 15 to 20 minutes to chill.

2 In blender or food processor, place chilled soymilk, peaches and honey. Cover; blend on high speed about 1 minute or until smooth. Pour into 2 glasses. Serve immediately.

1 Serving: Calories 330; Total Fat 3g (Saturated Fat 0.5g; Trans Fat 0g); Cholesterol 0mg; Sodium 200mg; Total Carbohydrate 68g (Dietary Fiber 5g); Protein 8g   **Exchanges:** 1½ Fruit, 2½ Other Carbohydrate, 1 Skim Milk   **Carbohydrate Choices:** 4½

orange frosties

PREP TIME: 5 Minutes • **START TO FINISH:** 5 Minutes • 4 servings (1 cup each)

2   cups ice cubes or slightly crushed ice

2   cups vanilla soymilk

1   can (6 oz) frozen orange juice concentrate

1 In blender or food processor, place all ingredients. Cover; blend on high speed 30 to 60 seconds or until smooth and frothy.

2 Pour into 4 glasses. Serve immediately.

1 Serving: Calories 120; Total Fat 1.5g (Saturated Fat 0g; Trans Fat 0g); Cholesterol 0mg; Sodium 85mg; Total Carbohydrate 22g (Dietary Fiber 0g); Protein 4g **Exchanges:** 1 Other Carbohydrate, ½ Low-Fat Milk **Carbohydrate Choices:** 1½

mix it up

Jazz up the glasses with a garnish of an orange slice and a sprig of fresh mint.

tropical papaya smoothies

PREP TIME: 10 Minutes • **START TO FINISH:** 10 Minutes • 2 servings (1½ cups each)

½ medium papaya, peeled, seeded and chopped (¾ cup)

½ cup frozen unsweetened whole strawberries

½ cup fat-free (skim) milk

½ cup plain fat-free yogurt

1 tablespoon honey

3 large ice cubes

Sliced papaya or sliced fresh strawberries, if desired

Fresh mint leaves or sprigs, if desired

1 In blender, place chopped papaya, frozen strawberries, milk, yogurt and honey. Cover; blend on high speed until smooth. With blender running, add ice cubes, one at a time, blending until ice is crushed and mixture is smooth.

2 Pour into 2 tall glasses. Garnish with sliced papaya or fresh strawberries and mint. Serve immediately.

1 Serving: Calories 150; Total Fat 0g (Saturated Fat 0g; Trans Fat 0g); Cholesterol 0mg; Sodium 80mg; Total Carbohydrate 30g (Dietary Fiber 2g); Protein 6g **Exchanges:** ½ Starch, 1 Fruit, ½ Skim Milk **Carbohydrate Choices:** 2

watermelon-kiwi-banana smoothies

PREP TIME: 10 Minutes • **START TO FINISH:** 10 Minutes • 2 servings (1 cup each)

1   cup coarsely chopped seeded watermelon

1   kiwifruit, peeled, cut into pieces

2   ice cubes

1   banana, frozen, peeled and cut into chunks

¼   cup chilled apple juice

1 In blender, place all ingredients. Cover; blend on high speed about 30 seconds or until smooth.

2 Pour into 2 glasses. Serve immediately.

1 Serving: Calories 130; Total Fat 0.5g (Saturated Fat 0g; Trans Fat 0g); Cholesterol 0mg; Sodium 0mg; Total Carbohydrate 29g (Dietary Fiber 3g); Protein 1g   **Exchanges:** 1 Fruit, 1 Other Carbohydrate   **Carbohydrate Choices:** 2

Veggie Smoothies

easy-being-green smoothies

PREP TIME: 10 Minutes • **START TO FINISH:** 10 Minutes • 2 servings (1 cup each)

1 box (9 oz) frozen chopped spinach

1 container (6 oz) Key lime pie low-fat yogurt

2 medium kiwifruit, peeled, quartered

½ cup ice cubes

⅓ cup apple juice

1 Microwave spinach as directed on box.* Rinse with cold water until cooled. Drain well, squeezing out as much liquid as possible.

2 In blender, place ⅓ cup of the cooked spinach and remaining ingredients. (Cover and refrigerate remaining spinach for another use.) Cover; blend on high speed about 30 seconds or until smooth.

3 Pour into 2 glasses. Serve immediately.

1 Serving: Calories 160; Total Fat 1.5g (Saturated Fat 0.5g; Trans Fat 0g); Cholesterol 5mg; Sodium 60mg; Total Carbohydrate 32g (Dietary Fiber 3g); Protein 4g **Exchanges:** 1½ Fruit, ½ Skim Milk, 1 Vegetable **Carbohydrate Choices:** 2

* For food safety reasons, frozen vegetables must be cooked.

mix it up

For the coolest smoothies, start with refrigerated fruit and juice.

beginner green spinach smoothies

PREP TIME: 10 Minutes • **START TO FINISH:** 10 Minutes • 2 servings (1 cup each)

1   box (9 oz) frozen
    chopped spinach

1   medium banana, cut up

1¼ cups frozen
    whole strawberries

¾   cup orange juice

1 Microwave spinach as directed on box.* Rinse with cold water until cooled. Drain well, squeezing out as much liquid as possible.

2 In blender, place ¼ cup of the cooked spinach and remaining ingredients. (Cover and refrigerate remaining spinach for another use.) Cover; blend on high speed about 30 seconds or until smooth.

3 Pour into 2 glasses. Serve immediately.

1 Serving: Calories 170; Total Fat 0.5g (Saturated Fat 0g; Trans Fat 0g); Cholesterol 0mg; Sodium 30mg; Total Carbohydrate 38g (Dietary Fiber 5g); Protein 2g   **Exchanges:** ½ Starch, 1½ Fruit, ½ Other Carbohydrate   **Carbohydrate Choices:** 2½

* For food safety reasons, frozen vegetables must be cooked.

mix it up

While fresh strawberries can be used in this recipe, we like using frozen berries to make the smoothies thicker and colder.

super-athlete spinach smoothies

PREP TIME: 10 Minutes • **START TO FINISH:** 10 Minutes • 2 servings (1 cup each)

1 box (9 oz) frozen chopped spinach

1 container (6 oz) blueberry Greek yogurt

½ ripe avocado, pitted, peeled

¾ cup cranberry-blueberry juice

½ cup frozen blueberries

1 Microwave spinach as directed on box.* Rinse with cold water until cooled. Drain well, squeezing out as much liquid as possible.

2 In blender, place ¼ cup of the cooked spinach and remaining ingredients. (Cover and refrigerate remaining spinach for another use.) Cover; blend on high speed about 30 seconds or until smooth.

3 Pour into 2 glasses. Serve immediately.

1 Serving: Calories 230; Total Fat 6g (Saturated Fat 1g; Trans Fat 0g); Cholesterol 5mg; Sodium 75mg; Total Carbohydrate 36g (Dietary Fiber 5g); Protein 8g **Exchanges:** 1½ Starch, ½ Fruit, ½ Skim Milk, 1 Fat **Carbohydrate Choices:** 2½

* For food safety reasons, frozen vegetables must be cooked.

mix it up

Here's an easy way to pit an avocado: Cut the avocado lengthwise in half around the pit, and twist apart the halves. The pit will stay in one of the halves. Firmly and carefully strike the pit with the sharp edge of a knife. While holding the avocado, twist the knife to loosen and remove the pit.

super spinach smoothies

PREP TIME: 5 Minutes • **START TO FINISH:** 5 Minutes • 2 servings (1 cup each)

1 cup fat-free (skim) milk

1 pouch (7.6 oz) triple berry–flavor pieces of frozen fruit and yogurt chips smoothie mix

½ cup packed torn fresh spinach

1 In blender, place all ingredients. Cover; blend on high speed 1 minute to 1 minute 30 seconds, stopping blender to scrape down sides as necessary, until smooth.

2 Pour into 2 glasses. Serve immediately.

1 Serving: Calories 120; Total Fat 1g (Saturated Fat 0g; Trans Fat 0g); Cholesterol 5mg; Sodium 75mg; Total Carbohydrate 20g (Dietary Fiber 2g); Protein 6g **Exchanges:** ½ Fruit, ½ Other Carbohydrate, ½ Skim Milk **Carbohydrate Choices:** 1

mix it up

To make this recipe super easy, purchase spinach that is washed.

sweet sensation spinach smoothies

PREP TIME: 10 Minutes • **START TO FINISH:** 10 Minutes • 2 servings (1 cup each)

1 box (9 oz) frozen chopped spinach

1 medium banana, cut up

1 cup frozen sliced peaches

½ cup lime sherbet

½ cup pineapple juice

1 Microwave spinach as directed on box.* Rinse with cold water until cooled. Drain well, squeezing out as much liquid as possible.

2 In blender, place ¼ cup of the cooked spinach and remaining ingredients. (Cover and refrigerate remaining spinach for another use.) Cover; blend on high speed about 30 seconds or until smooth.

3 Pour into 2 glasses. Serve immediately.

1 Serving: Calories 190; Total Fat 1.5g (Saturated Fat 0.5g; Trans Fat 0g); Cholesterol 0mg; Sodium 45mg; Total Carbohydrate 42g (Dietary Fiber 4g); Protein 2g **Exchanges:** ½ Starch, 1 Fruit, 1½ Other Carbohydrate, ½ Fat **Carbohydrate Choices:** 3

* For food safety reasons, frozen vegetables must be cooked.

mix it up

If your blender doesn't handle frozen fruit very well, thaw the peaches slightly before adding them to the blender.

everything-but-the-kitchen-sink smoothies

PREP TIME: 10 Minutes • **START TO FINISH:** 10 Minutes • 2 servings (1 cup each)

½ cup almond milk

3 cups packed fresh baby spinach

2 tablespoons lemon juice

1 tablespoon honey

1 banana, chopped, frozen

½ cup ice cubes

1 In blender, place all ingredients. Cover; blend on high speed until smooth.

2 Pour into 2 glasses. Serve immediately.

1 Serving: Calories 130; Total Fat 1g (Saturated Fat 0g; Trans Fat 0g); Cholesterol 0mg; Sodium 75mg; Total Carbohydrate 27g (Dietary Fiber 3g); Protein 2g **Exchanges:** ½ Fruit, 1 Other Carbohydrate, 1 Vegetable **Carbohydrate Choices:** 2

mix it up

If you are not a fan of almond milk, try using soymilk or rice or hemp milk instead.

Substitute ⅔ cup frozen mango chunks for the frozen banana.

nutritious green smoothies

PREP TIME: 10 Minutes • **START TO FINISH:** 10 Minutes • 3 servings (1½ cups each)

2 cups coconut water, chilled

3 cups packed fresh baby spinach leaves

3 celery stalks, chopped (1 cup)

1 Granny Smith apple, cored, seeded and chopped

1 medium banana, frozen

½ lemon, peeled, seeded

½ cup fresh parsley leaves

1 ripe avocado, pitted, peeled

1 piece (1 inch) gingerroot, peeled, chopped

1 In blender, place all ingredients. Cover; blend on medium-high speed until very smooth.

2 Pour into 3 glasses. Serve immediately.

1 Serving: Calories 210; Total Fat 8g (Saturated Fat 1.5g; Trans Fat 0g); Cholesterol 0mg; Sodium 230mg; Total Carbohydrate 31g (Dietary Fiber 9g); Protein 4g **Exchanges:** ½ Starch, 1 Fruit, 1 Vegetable, 1½ Fat **Carbohydrate Choices:** 2

mix it up

If you don't like the texture of celery, remove the strings before chopping. This will result in a much smoother drink.

triple berry and spinach smoothies

PREP TIME: 10 Minutes • **START TO FINISH:** 10 Minutes • 4 servings (1 cup each)

1 cup canned reduced-fat (lite) coconut milk (not cream of coconut)

½ cup orange juice

¼ cup lime juice

¼ cup water

1 bag (10 oz) frozen harvest berries (strawberries, blackberries and blueberries)

1 cup packed fresh baby spinach leaves

¼ cup Fiber One™ original bran cereal

2 tablespoons flaxseed

1 medium banana

1 In blender, place all ingredients. Cover; blend on high speed 30 to 45 seconds, stopping occasionally to scrape down sides as necessary, until flaxseed and spinach are finely chopped.

2 Pour into 4 glasses. Serve immediately.

1 Serving: Calories 170; Total Fat 6g (Saturated Fat 3.5g; Trans Fat 0g); Cholesterol 0mg; Sodium 45mg; Total Carbohydrate 27g (Dietary Fiber 6g); Protein 2g **Exchanges:** ½ Starch, ½ Fruit, 1 Other Carbohydrate, 1 Fat **Carbohydrate Choices:** 2

mix it up

For sweeter smoothies, add 2 to 3 teaspoons agave nectar to the mixture in the blender.

Coconut milk can separate a bit while in the can, so be sure to stir it before measuring.

green goodness smoothies

PREP TIME: 5 Minutes • **START TO FINISH:** 5 Minutes • 4 servings (1 cup each)

1 cup pear nectar

2 cups loosely packed chopped fresh spinach

½ cup chopped seeded peeled cucumber

½ cup plain fat-free yogurt

2 tablespoons honey

2 cups ice cubes

1 In blender, place all ingredients. Cover; blend on high speed about 1 minute or until smooth.

2 Pour into 4 glasses. Serve immediately.

1 Serving: Calories 100; Total Fat 0.5g (Saturated Fat 0g; Trans Fat 0g); Cholesterol 0mg; Sodium 40mg; Total Carbohydrate 22g (Dietary Fiber 1g); Protein 2g **Exchanges:** ½ Starch, 1 Other Carbohydrate, ½ Vegetable **Carbohydrate Choices:** 1½

boost it

Get a nutritional boost by adding a tablespoon of flaxseed with the other ingredients. Be sure to blend long enough to grind up the flaxseed.

berry-cucumber smoothies

PREP TIME: 10 Minutes • **START TO FINISH:** 10 Minutes • 2 servings

1 cup fat-free (skim) milk

¾ cup cubed sliced cucumber

½ ripe avocado, pitted, peeled

1 pouch (7.6 oz) triple berry–flavor pieces of frozen fruit and yogurt chips smoothie mix

1 In blender, place all ingredients. Cover; blend on high speed 1 minute to 1 minute 30 seconds, stopping to scrape down sides as necessary, until smooth.

2 Pour into 2 glasses. Serve immediately.

1 Serving: Calories 190; Total Fat 7g (Saturated Fat 1g; Trans Fat 0g); Cholesterol 0mg; Sodium 85mg; Total Carbohydrate 25g (Dietary Fiber 5g); Protein 7g **Exchanges:** ½ Fruit, 1 Skim Milk, ½ Vegetable, 1 Fat **Carbohydrate Choices:** 1½

mix it up

Avocados are often picked while still firm, which is often how they arrive in the supermarket. Let them stand at room temperature for a few days to ripen. Speed up the ripening by placing the avocados in a paper bag. Ripe avocados will give slightly when pressed with your thumb.

pea perfection smoothies

PREP TIME: 10 Minutes • **START TO FINISH:** 10 Minutes • 2 servings (1 cup each)

1 bag (12 oz) frozen
  sweet peas

1 cup frozen
  whole strawberries

½ cup pineapple juice

1 medium banana, cut up

1 Cook peas as directed on bag.* Rinse with cold water until cooled. Drain.

2 In blender, place ⅓ cup of the cooked peas and remaining ingredients. (Cover and refrigerate remaining peas for another use.) Cover; blend on high speed about 30 seconds or until smooth.

3 Pour into 2 glasses. Serve immediately.

1 Serving: Calories 190; Total Fat 0.5g (Saturated Fat 0g; Trans Fat 0g); Cholesterol 0mg; Sodium 25mg; Total Carbohydrate 43g (Dietary Fiber 5g); Protein 3g **Exchanges:** 1 Starch, 1 Fruit, 1 Other Carbohydrate **Carbohydrate Choices:** 3

* For food safety reasons, frozen vegetables must be cooked.

mix it up

Use the remaining cooked peas in a
mixed greens salad, or add them to a soup
or stir-fry.

asian kale smoothies

PREP TIME: 10 Minutes • **START TO FINISH:** 10 Minutes • 2 servings

1 container (5.3 oz)
   100-calorie vanilla
   Greek yogurt

1 cup coarsely chopped
   fresh kale leaves

¼ cup orange juice

2 tablespoons lemon juice

2 tablespoons honey

1 banana, cut in half

1 teaspoon freshly
   grated gingerroot

¼ teaspoon ground nutmeg

1 In blender, place all ingredients. Cover; blend on high speed 30 to 45 seconds, stopping blender to scrape down sides as necessary.

2 Pour into 2 glasses. Serve immediately.

1 Serving: Calories 220; Total Fat 0.5g (Saturated Fat 0g; Trans Fat 0g); Cholesterol 0mg; Sodium 45mg; Total Carbohydrate 45g (Dietary Fiber 2g); Protein 8g **Exchanges:** ½ Fruit, 2 Other Carbohydrate, ½ Skim Milk, ½ Very Lean Meat **Carbohydrate Choices:** 3

mix it up

Wash and chop the kale ahead of time and store it in resealable food-storage plastic bags in the refrigerator. It'll make blending these smoothies a breeze in the morning.

kale-berry smoothies

PREP TIME: 10 Minutes • **START TO FINISH:** 10 Minutes • 2 servings

1 container (5.3 oz) 100-calorie mixed berry Greek yogurt

1 cup coarsely chopped kale leaves

¼ cup orange juice

10 fresh mint leaves

2 tablespoons lemon juice

2 tablespoons honey

1 cup frozen organic harvest berries (strawberries, blackberries and blueberries), from 10-oz bag

1 In blender, place all ingredients. Cover; blend on high speed 30 to 45 seconds, stopping blender to scrape down sides as necessary.

2 Pour into 2 glasses. Serve immediately.

1 Serving: Calories 210; Total Fat 0.5g (Saturated Fat 0g; Trans Fat 0g); Cholesterol 0mg; Sodium 40mg; Total Carbohydrate 44g (Dietary Fiber 4g); Protein 7g **Exchanges:** ½ Fruit, 2 Other Carbohydrate, ½ Skim Milk, ½ Very Lean Meat **Carbohydrate Choices:** 3

boost it

If you want to add more fruit to the smoothies, try adding a banana to the blender mixture. You'll get the added value of the fruit and the smoothies will be a little thicker too.

spa refreshers

PREP TIME: 10 Minutes • **START TO FINISH:** 10 Minutes • 2 servings (1 cup each)

1 bag (12 oz) frozen broccoli cuts

½ cup English (hothouse) cucumber slices

1 container (6 oz) Key lime pie low-fat yogurt

½ cup pineapple juice

½ cup crushed ice cubes

1 Cook broccoli as directed on bag.* Rinse with cold water until cooled. Drain.

2 In blender, place ¼ cup of the cooked broccoli and remaining ingredients. (Cover and refrigerate remaining broccoli for another use.) Cover; blend on high speed about 30 seconds or until smooth.

3 Pour into 2 glasses. Serve immediately.

1 Serving: Calories 100; Total Fat 0g (Saturated Fat 0g; Trans Fat 0g); Cholesterol 0mg; Sodium 40mg; Total Carbohydrate 20g (Dietary Fiber 1g); Protein 3g **Exchanges:** 1 Other Carbohydrate, ½ Skim Milk **Carbohydrate Choices:** 1

* For food safety reasons, frozen vegetables must be cooked.

mix it up

English cucumbers are virtually seedless, so they are great for smoothies. If stored whole and unwashed, cucumbers will keep up to 10 days in the refrigerator.

broccoli power-punch smoothies

PREP TIME: 10 Minutes • **START TO FINISH:** 10 Minutes • 2 servings (1 cup each)

1 bag (12 oz) frozen broccoli cuts

1 cup frozen unsweetened mango chunks

½ cup frozen unsweetened whole strawberries

1 medium banana, cut up

½ cup pineapple juice

1 Cook broccoli as directed on bag.* Rinse with cold water until cooled. Drain.

2 In blender, place ⅓ cup of the cooked broccoli and remaining ingredients. (Cover and refrigerate remaining broccoli for another use.) Cover; blend on high speed about 30 seconds or until smooth.

3 Pour into 2 glasses. Serve immediately.

1 Serving: Calories 180; Total Fat 0.5g (Saturated Fat 0g; Trans Fat 0g); Cholesterol 0mg; Sodium 5mg; Total Carbohydrate 41g (Dietary Fiber 5g); Protein 2g **Exchanges:** ½ Starch, 1 Fruit, 1 Other Carbohydrate **Carbohydrate Choices:** 3

* For food safety reasons, frozen vegetables must be cooked.

mix it up

Keep frozen mango on hand for smoothies. Besides adding flavor and thickness to your smoothies, it saves time since the mango is already peeled and cut into cubes.

broccoli-banana-blueberry smoothies

PREP TIME: 10 Minutes • **START TO FINISH:** 10 Minutes • 2 servings

½ cup frozen broccoli cuts (from 9-oz box)

1 cup fat-free (skim) milk

½ medium banana

1 pouch (7.6 oz) blueberry-pomegranate-flavor pieces of frozen fruit and yogurt chips smoothie mix

1 Cook broccoli as directed on box.* Rinse with cold water until cooled. Drain.

2 In blender, place all ingredients. Cover; blend on high speed 1 minute to 1 minute 30 seconds, stopping to scrape down sides as necessary, until smooth.

3 Pour into 2 glasses. Serve immediately.

1 Serving: Calories 200; Total Fat 2g (Saturated Fat 0g; Trans Fat 0g); Cholesterol 0mg; Sodium 85mg; Total Carbohydrate 37g (Dietary Fiber 4g); Protein 8g **Exchanges:** ½ Fruit, 1 Other Carbohydrate, 1 Skim Milk **Carbohydrate Choices:** 2½

* For food safety reasons, frozen vegetables must be cooked.

mix it up

Look for the smoothie mix in the freezer section of your grocery store, usually near the frozen fruit.

tropical power smoothies

PREP TIME: 10 Minutes • **START TO FINISH:** 10 Minutes • 2 servings (1 cup each)

1   bag (12 oz) frozen broccoli cuts

½   cup frozen blueberries

½   ripe avocado, pitted, peeled

⅔   cup water

½   cup coconut milk (not cream of coconut)

2   teaspoons sugar

1 Cook broccoli as directed on bag.* Rinse with cold water until cooled. Drain.

2 In blender, place ¼ cup of the cooked broccoli and remaining ingredients. (Cover and refrigerate remaining broccoli for another use.) Cover; blend on high speed about 30 seconds or until smooth.

3 Pour into 2 glasses. Serve immediately.

1 Serving: Calories 240; Total Fat 17g (Saturated Fat 11g; Trans Fat 0g); Cholesterol 0mg; Sodium 15mg; Total Carbohydrate 19g (Dietary Fiber 5g); Protein 2g   **Exchanges:** ½ Starch, ½ Fruit, ½ Other Carbohydrate, 3½ Fat   **Carbohydrate Choices:** 1

* For food safety reasons, frozen vegetables must be cooked.

mix it up

You can use reduced-fat coconut milk, but the smoothies may be slightly less thick. Leftover coconut milk can be frozen in small quantities for future uses.

triple-treat antioxidant smoothies

PREP TIME: 10 Minutes • **START TO FINISH:** 10 Minutes • 2 servings (1 cup each)

1 bag (12 oz) frozen broccoli cuts

½ cup frozen whole strawberries

½ cup frozen red raspberries

½ cup pomegranate juice

⅓ cup vanilla low-fat yogurt (from 6-oz container)

1 teaspoon sugar

1 Cook broccoli as directed on bag.* Rinse with cold water until cooled. Drain.

2 In blender, place ¼ cup of the cooked broccoli and remaining ingredients. (Cover and refrigerate remaining broccoli for another use.) Cover; blend on high speed about 30 seconds or until smooth.

3 Pour into 2 glasses. Serve immediately.

1 Serving: Calories 150; Total Fat 1g (Saturated Fat 0g; Trans Fat 0g); Cholesterol 0mg; Sodium 35mg; Total Carbohydrate 32g (Dietary Fiber 6g); Protein 3g **Exchanges:** 1 Starch, 1 Fruit **Carbohydrate Choices:** 2

* For food safety reasons, frozen vegetables must be cooked.

mix it up

Look for pomegranate juice in single-serving bottles in delis or beverage machines, or in larger economy-size containers in the juice aisle of the grocery store.

strawberry-veggie smoothies

PREP TIME: 10 Minutes • **START TO FINISH:** 10 Minutes • 2 servings (1½ cups each)

1 bag (12 oz) frozen broccoli cuts

1 container (6 oz) French vanilla low-fat yogurt

½ ripe avocado, pitted, peeled

¾ cup pomegranate juice

1 cup frozen unsweetened whole strawberries

1 Cook broccoli as directed on bag.* Rinse with cold water until cooled. Drain well.

2 In blender, place ¼ cup of the cooked broccoli and remaining ingredients. (Cover and refrigerate remaining broccoli for another use.) Cover; blend on high speed about 30 seconds or until smooth.

3 Pour into 2 glasses. Serve immediately.

1 Serving: Calories 250; Total Fat 7g (Saturated Fat 1.5g; Trans Fat 0g); Cholesterol 0mg; Sodium 65mg; Total Carbohydrate 43g (Dietary Fiber 5g); Protein 5g **Exchanges:** ½ Starch, 2 Other Carbohydrate, ½ Skim Milk, 1 Fat **Carbohydrate Choices:** 3

* For food safety reasons, frozen vegetables must be cooked.

obviously orange smoothies

PREP TIME: 10 Minutes • **START TO FINISH:** 10 Minutes • 2 servings (1 cup each)

1 bag (12 oz) frozen broccoli cuts

1 cup frozen mango chunks

½ cup carrot juice

½ cup orange juice

1 tablespoon sugar

1 Cook broccoli as directed on bag.* Rinse with cold water until cooled. Drain.

2 In blender, place ¼ cup of the cooked broccoli and remaining ingredients. (Cover and refrigerate remaining broccoli for another use.) Cover; blend on high speed about 30 seconds or until smooth.

3 Pour into 2 glasses. Serve immediately.

1 Serving: Calories 140; Total Fat 0.5g (Saturated Fat 0g; Trans Fat 0g); Cholesterol 0mg; Sodium 20mg; Total Carbohydrate 32g (Dietary Fiber 2g); Protein 2g **Exchanges:** ½ Starch, 1 Fruit, ½ Other Carbohydrate **Carbohydrate Choices:** 2

* For food safety reasons, frozen vegetables must be cooked.

mix it up

Look for carrot juice in the refrigerated case of the produce section.

carrot-orange smoothies

PREP TIME: 5 Minutes • **START TO FINISH:** 5 Minutes • 2 servings

1 cup fat-free (skim) milk

1 cup ready-to-eat baby-cut carrots

1 orange or 2 clementines, peeled, quartered

1 pouch (7.6 oz) triple berry–flavor pieces of frozen fruit and yogurt chips smoothie mix

1 In blender, place all ingredients. Cover; blend on high speed 1 minute to 1 minute 30 seconds, stopping to scrape down sides as necessary, until smooth.

2 Pour into 2 glasses. Serve immediately.

1 Serving: Calories 180; Total Fat 2g (Saturated Fat 0g; Trans Fat 0g); Cholesterol 0mg; Sodium 125mg; Total Carbohydrate 34g (Dietary Fiber 5g); Protein 7g   **Exchanges:** ½ Fruit, 1 Other Carbohydrate, 1 Skim Milk, ½ Vegetable   **Carbohydrate Choices:** 2

mix it up

Substitute ½ cup canned mandarin oranges, drained, for the fresh orange. The flavor will be slightly sweeter.

Substitute 1 cup frozen sliced carrots, cooked and rinsed with cold water to cool, for the fresh baby-cut carrots. The smoothies will have a bit smoother texture.

sweet potato pie smoothies

PREP TIME: 5 Minutes • **START TO FINISH:** 5 Minutes • 2 servings (1 cup each)

1¼   cups milk

¼   cup cooked sweet potato, chilled

1   container (6 oz) French vanilla low-fat yogurt

1   tablespoon honey

¼   teaspoon ground cinnamon

¼   teaspoon vanilla

1 In blender or food processor, place all ingredients. Cover; blend on high speed about 1 minute or until smooth.

2 Pour into 2 glasses. Serve immediately.

1 Serving: Calories 220; Total Fat 4g (Saturated Fat 2.5g; Trans Fat 0g); Cholesterol 15mg; Sodium 190mg; Total Carbohydrate 35g (Dietary Fiber 1g); Protein 10g   **Exchanges:** 1½ Other Carbohydrate, 1 Skim Milk, ½ Fat   **Carbohydrate Choices:** 2

mix it up

What a great way to use up leftover cooked sweet potatoes!

Any vanilla-flavored yogurt can be used for this recipe.

pumpkin perfection protein smoothie shake

PREP TIME: 10 Minutes • START TO FINISH: 10 Minutes • 1 serving (2 cups)

½ cup canned pumpkin (not pumpkin pie mix)

¼ cup 100-calorie vanilla Greek yogurt

¼ cup milk

1 scoop vanilla protein powder (6 tablespoons)

2 tablespoons packed brown sugar

1 tablespoon ground flaxseed meal

1 tablespoon pumpkin pie spice

1 tablespoon vanilla

1 cup ice cubes

1 In blender, place all ingredients. Cover; blend on high speed until smooth.

2 Pour into large glass. Serve immediately.

1 Serving: Calories 470; Total Fat 7g (Saturated Fat 2g; Trans Fat 0g); Cholesterol 85mg; Sodium 170mg; Total Carbohydrate 60g (Dietary Fiber 7g); Protein 35g **Exchanges:** 1 Starch, 2 Other Carbohydrate, 1½ Skim Milk, 3 Very Lean Meat, ½ Fat **Carbohydrate Choices:** 4

Variation: For a fun alternative, use chocolate protein powder, and add 1 tablespoon unsweetened baking cocoa.

mix it up
Molasses makes a lovely bittersweet stand-in for the brown sugar.

Indulgent Smoothies

tropical smoothie

PREP TIME: 10 Minutes • **START TO FINISH:** 10 Minutes • 1 serving (1½ cups)

1 cup frozen pineapple chunks

1 banana, quartered

2 tablespoons lime juice

1 container (5.3 oz) blended coconut Greek yogurt

½ teaspoon rum extract, if desired

1 In blender, place all ingredients. Cover; blend on high speed until smooth.

2 Pour into glass. Serve immediately.

1 Serving: Calories 360; Total Fat 1.5g (Saturated Fat 0.5g; Trans Fat 0g); Cholesterol 0mg; Sodium 60mg; Total Carbohydrate 74g (Dietary Fiber 5g); Protein 13g **Exchanges:** ½ Starch, 1½ Fruit, 2 Other Carbohydrate, 1 Skim Milk, ½ Very Lean Meat **Carbohydrate Choices:** 5

mix it up

Frozen mango makes a nice stand-in for the pineapple in this recipe.

key lime–banana smoothies

PREP TIME: 10 Minutes • START TO FINISH: 10 Minutes • 2 servings (1 cup each)

1 container (6 oz) Key lime pie low-fat yogurt

1 ripe banana, sliced

½ cup milk

1 tablespoon lime juice

¼ teaspoon dry lemon-lime-flavor soft drink mix (from 0.13-oz package)

1 cup vanilla frozen yogurt

1 In blender, place yogurt, banana, milk, lime juice and soft drink mix. Cover; blend on high speed until smooth. Add frozen yogurt; cover and blend until smooth.

2 Pour into 2 glasses. Serve immediately.

1 Serving: Calories 340; Total Fat 4.5g (Saturated Fat 2.5g; Trans Fat 0g); Cholesterol 15mg; Sodium 160mg; Total Carbohydrate 64g (Dietary Fiber 2g); Protein 12g **Exchanges:** 2½ Fruit, 1 Low-Fat Milk, 1 Fat **Carbohydrate Choices:** 4

mix it up

For the best banana flavor, choose bananas that have flecks of brown on the skin. Bananas that are too green will not beas sweet or flavorful.

Decorate the rim of each glass with a fresh slice of lime.

papaya colada coolers

PREP TIME: 15 Minutes • **START TO FINISH:** 15 Minutes • 4 servings

1 medium papaya

1 can (8 oz) crushed pineapple in unsweetened juice, undrained

2 cups creamy vanilla low-fat yogurt (from 2-lb container)

½ cup orange juice

¾ teaspoon coconut extract

1½ cups crushed ice

1 Cut papaya in half; scoop out and discard seeds. Scoop flesh from skin into food processor bowl with metal blade. Add pineapple with juice; process until smooth. Add yogurt, orange juice, extract and crushed ice; process until smooth.

2 Pour into 4 glasses. Serve immediately.

1 Serving: Calories 190; Total Fat 1g (Saturated Fat 0.5g; Trans Fat 0g); Cholesterol 0mg; Sodium 60mg; Total Carbohydrate 39g (Dietary Fiber 2g); Protein 4g **Exchanges:** ½ Fruit, 2 Other Carbohydrate, ½ Skim Milk **Carbohydrate Choices:** 2½

taste-of-the-tropics smoothies

PREP TIME: 5 Minutes • **START TO FINISH:** 5 Minutes • 2 servings (1 cup each)

1 cup light coconut milk

1 pouch (7.6 oz) strawberry-mango-pineapple-flavor pieces of frozen fruit and yogurt chips smoothie mix

⅛ teaspoon ground ginger

1 In blender, place all ingredients. Cover; blend on high speed 1 minute to 1 minute 30 seconds, stopping blender to scrape down sides as necessary, until smooth.

2 Pour into 2 glasses. Serve immediately.

1 Serving: Calories 140; Total Fat 7g (Saturated Fat 6g; Trans Fat 0g); Cholesterol 0mg; Sodium 80mg; Total Carbohydrate 18g (Dietary Fiber 1g); Protein 1g **Exchanges:** ½ Starch, ½ Other Carbohydrate, 1½ Fat **Carbohydrate Choices:** 1

mix it up

If you want to punch up the flavor of the ginger, increase it to ¼ teaspoon.

creamy mango smoothies

PREP TIME: 10 Minutes • **START TO FINISH:** 10 Minutes • 6 servings (1 cup each)

2 mangoes, seeds removed, peeled and chopped (2 cups)

2 cups mango sorbet

2 containers (6 oz each) French vanilla low-fat yogurt

1½ cups fat-free (skim) milk or soymilk

1 In blender, place all ingredients. Cover; blend on high speed until smooth.

2 Pour into 6 glasses. Serve immediately.

1 Serving: Calories 200; Total Fat 1g (Saturated Fat 0.5g; Trans Fat 0g); Cholesterol 0mg; Sodium 70mg; Total Carbohydrate 42g (Dietary Fiber 1g); Protein 5g **Exchanges:** 2½ Other Carbohydrate, ½ Skim Milk **Carbohydrate Choices:** 3

boost it

Mango adds vitamins A and C, and the yogurt and milk add calcium and vitamin D to the smoothies.

mix it up

For the best flavor and color, choose ripe mangoes; look for skins that are yellow with blushes of red.

pink cabanas

PREP TIME: 5 Minutes • **START TO FINISH:** 5 Minutes • 2 servings (1⅓ cups each)

½ cup milk

½ cup pineapple juice

½ cup orange-flavor liqueur

1 pouch (7.6 oz) strawberry-banana-flavor pieces of frozen fruit and yogurt chips smoothie mix

1 In blender, place all ingredients. Cover; blend on high speed 1 minute to 1 minute 30 seconds, stopping blender to scrape down sides as necessary, until smooth.

2 Pour into 2 glasses. Serve immediately.

1 Serving: Calories 300; Total Fat 2.5g (Saturated Fat 1g; Trans Fat 0g); Cholesterol 0mg; Sodium 60mg; Total Carbohydrate 44g (Dietary Fiber 1g); Protein 3g   **Carbohydrate Choices:** 3

mix it up

Make it your way! For a less creamy cocktail, omit the milk and up the pineapple juice to ¾ cup.

For a drink without alcohol, omit the liqueur and replace with ½ cup orange juice.

mai tai smoothie

PREP TIME: 10 Minutes • **START TO FINISH:** 10 Minutes • 1 serving (1¾ cups)

¾   cup frozen pineapple

½   cup frozen cherries

½   cup orange juice

2   tablespoons lime juice

½   cup almond milk

1 In blender, place all ingredients. Cover; blend on high speed until smooth.

2 Pour into large glass. Serve immediately.

1 Serving: Calories 220; Total Fat 2g (Saturated Fat 0g; Trans Fat 0g); Cholesterol 0mg; Sodium 80mg; Total Carbohydrate 48g (Dietary Fiber 4g); Protein 3g   **Exchanges:** 2 Fruit, 1 Other Carbohydrate, ½ Skim Milk   **Carbohydrate Choices:** 3

mix it up

If you have fresh pineapple or cherries on hand, feel free to use them instead of frozen fruit. To keep the mixture icy, add ½ cup ice cubes.

These smoothies make an excellent nonalcoholic cocktail alternative for guests.

peach mojito smoothies

PREP TIME: 10 Minutes • **START TO FINISH:** 10 Minutes • 2 servings (1 cup each)

2 cups frozen peaches

2 tablespoons honey

½ cup plain fat-free yogurt

½ cup orange juice

1 tablespoon chopped fresh mint leaves

¼ cup almond milk

1 In blender, place all ingredients. Cover; blend on high speed until smooth.

2 Pour into 2 glasses. Serve immediately.

1 Serving: Calories 210; Total Fat 0.5g (Saturated Fat 0g; Trans Fat 0g); Cholesterol 0mg; Sodium 75mg; Total Carbohydrate 46g (Dietary Fiber 3g); Protein 5g **Exchanges:** ½ Starch, 1 Fruit, 1 Other Carbohydrate, ½ Skim Milk **Carbohydrate Choices:** 3

mix it up

For a pretty presentation and extra flavor, top the smoothies with a little extra shredded mint.

peachy chai smoothies

PREP TIME: 10 Minutes • **START TO FINISH:** 10 Minutes • 3 servings (1 cup each)

2 fresh peaches, peeled, pitted and sliced

2 containers (6 oz each) vanilla thick-and-creamy low-fat yogurt

⅓ cup chai tea latte mix (from 10-oz package)

½ cup milk

Ground nutmeg, if desired

1 In blender or food processor, place peaches, yogurt, latte mix and milk. Cover; blend on high speed about 1 minute or until smooth and creamy.

2 Pour into 3 glasses. Sprinkle each with dash of nutmeg. Serve immediately.

1 Serving: Calories 230; Total Fat 3.5g (Saturated Fat 1g; Trans Fat 0g); Cholesterol 10mg; Sodium 190mg; Total Carbohydrate 43g (Dietary Fiber 2g); Protein 9g **Exchanges:** 1½ Starch, 1 Fruit, ½ Skim Milk **Carbohydrate Choices:** 3

mix it up

For the sweetest smoothies with lots of peach flavor, use peaches that are very ripe.

luscious lemon drop smoothies

PREP TIME: 10 Minutes • **START TO FINISH:** 10 Minutes • **2 servings (1 cup each)**

1 bag (12 oz) frozen broccoli cuts

1 medium banana, cut up

1 cup frozen sliced peaches (from 10-oz bag)

¾ cup pineapple-orange juice

½ cup lemon sherbet

1 Cook broccoli as directed on bag.* Rinse with cold water until cooled. Drain.

2 In blender, place ¼ cup of the cooked broccoli and remaining ingredients. (Cover and refrigerate remaining broccoli for another use.) Cover; blend on high speed about 30 seconds or until smooth.

3 Pour into 2 glasses. Serve immediately.

1 Serving: Calories 200; Total Fat 1g (Saturated Fat 0.5g; Trans Fat 0g); Cholesterol 0mg; Sodium 25mg; Total Carbohydrate 45g (Dietary Fiber 4g); Protein 2g **Exchanges:** ½ Starch, 1 Fruit, 1½ Other Carbohydrate **Carbohydrate Choices:** 3

* For food safety reasons, frozen vegetables must be cooked.

mix it up

If you can't find pineapple-orange juice, just substitute pineapple juice.

blueberry bootleggers

PREP TIME: 5 Minutes • **START TO FINISH:** 5 Minutes • 2 servings (1 cup each)

¾   cup milk

¼   cup light rum

1   tablespoon lime juice

1   pouch (7.6 oz) blueberry-
pomegranate-flavor pieces
of frozen fruit and yogurt
chips smoothie mix

1 In blender, place all ingredients. Cover; blend on high speed 1 minute to 1 minute 30 seconds, stopping blender to scrape down sides as necessary, until smooth.

2 Pour into 2 glasses. Serve immediately.

1 Serving: Calories 200; Total Fat 3.5g (Saturated Fat 1g; Trans Fat 0g); Cholesterol 5mg; Sodium 75mg; Total Carbohydrate 21g (Dietary Fiber 2g); Protein 5g **Exchanges:** N/A **Carbohydrate Choices:** 1½

mix it up

For a drink without alcohol, omit the rum and increase the milk to 1 cup.

Chill the glasses in the freezer at least 15 minutes for extra-frosty smoothies!

berry cheesecake smoothies

PREP TIME: 10 Minutes • **START TO FINISH:** 10 Minutes • 4 servings

1 bag (12 oz) frozen mixed berries

2 cups fat-free (skim) milk

⅔ cup cream cheese frosting (from 16-oz container)

¼ cup triple berry preserves

1⅓ cups whipped cream topping (from aerosol can)

1 teaspoon graham cracker crumbs

1 Reserve 12 frozen blueberries from the mixed berries for garnish. In blender, place remaining mixed berries, the milk, frosting and preserves. Cover; blend on medium-high speed 30 seconds, stopping once to scrape sides, until smooth.

2 Pour into 4 glasses. Top with whipped cream topping, graham cracker crumbs and reserved frozen blueberries.

1 Serving: Calories 390; Total Fat 12g (Saturated Fat 5g); Sodium 170mg; Total Carbohydrate 66g (Dietary Fiber 4g); Protein 5g **Exchanges:** ½ Starch, ½ Fruit, 3 Other Carbohydrate, ½ Skim Milk, 2 Fat **Carbohydrate Choices:** 4½

apple turnover smoothies

PREP TIME: 10 Minutes • **START TO FINISH:** 10 Minutes • 2 servings

2   containers (6 oz each) apple turnover fat-free yogurt

½   cup unsweetened applesauce

1   cup chopped apple

Apple pie spice

Apple slices

1 In blender, place yogurt, applesauce and chopped apple. Cover; blend on medium speed until smooth.

2 Pour into 2 glasses. Top with apple pie spice and apple slice.

1 Serving: Calories 170; Total Fat 0g (Saturated Fat 0g; Trans Fat 0g); Cholesterol 0mg; Sodium 85mg; Total Carbohydrate 36g (Dietary Fiber 2g); Protein 5g   **Exchanges:** 2 Other Carbohydrate, ½ Skim Milk   **Carbohydrate Choices:** 2½

pumpkin pie yogurt smoothies

PREP TIME: 5 Minutes • **START TO FINISH:** 5 Minutes • 2 servings (1 cup each)

1 container (6 oz) pumpkin pie fat-free yogurt

1 cup crushed ice

½ cup pumpkin pie mix (not plain pumpkin)

¼ cup fat-free (skim) milk

2 tablespoons fat-free whipped topping

Pumpkin pie spice

1 In blender or food processor, place yogurt, ice, pumpkin pie mix and milk. Cover; blend on high speed about 1 minute or until smooth.

2 Pour into 2 glasses. Top each with whipped topping and dash of pumpkin pie spice. Serve immediately.

1 Serving: Calories 130; Total Fat 2g (Saturated Fat 1g; Trans Fat 0g); Cholesterol 30mg; Sodium 160mg; Total Carbohydrate 22g (Dietary Fiber 1g); Protein 6g   **Exchanges:** 1½ Starch, ½ Fat   **Carbohydrate Choices:** 1½

mix it up

This is a great way to use any leftover canned pumpkin pie mix. Canned pumpkin and pumpkin pie mix freeze well, so be sure to freeze any leftovers.

chilling jack-o'-lantern smoothies

PREP TIME: 15 Minutes • **START TO FINISH:** 15 Minutes • 4 servings (¾ cup each)

1 tablespoon semisweet
  chocolate chips

4 plastic cups (8 to
  9 oz each)

3 containers (6 oz each)
  orange crème or peach
  low-fat yogurt

¼ cup frozen (thawed) orange
  juice concentrate

1 can (11 oz) mandarin
  orange segments, chilled,
  drained

1 banana, sliced

1 In small microwavable bowl, microwave chocolate chips on High 1 minute or until melted. With tip of knife, spread chocolate on inside of 1 plastic cup to resemble eyes, nose and mouth of jack-o'-lantern. Repeat with remaining 3 cups. Refrigerate 5 minutes or until chocolate is set.

2 Meanwhile, in blender, place remaining ingredients. Cover; blend until smooth. Pour into chocolate-painted cups. Serve immediately.

1 Serving: Calories 230; Total Fat 2g (Saturated Fat 1.5g; Trans Fat 0g); Cholesterol 10mg; Sodium 65mg; Total Carbohydrate 47g (Dietary Fiber 2g); Protein 5g **Exchanges:** ½ Fruit, 2½ Other Carbohydrate, ½ Skim Milk **Carbohydrate Choices:** 3

mix it up

It works best to place the cup on its side
when painting the face.

Serve with a green straw to resemble a
pumpkin stem or garnish with a mint leaf.

french silk protein smoothie shake

PREP TIME: 10 Minutes • **START TO FINISH:** 10 Minutes • 1 serving (1¾ cups)

1   scoop chocolate protein powder (6 tablespoons)

1   tablespoon ground flaxseed meal

1   cup chocolate-flavor almond milk

½   cup ice cubes

1   tablespoon unsweetened baking cocoa

1   teaspoon vanilla

1   tablespoon frozen (thawed) fat-free whipped topping

1   tablespoon graham cracker crumbs

1   teaspoon grated bittersweet baking chocolate

1 In blender, place protein powder, flaxseed meal, almond milk, ice cubes, cocoa and vanilla. Cover; blend on high speed until smooth.

2 Pour into large glass. Top with remaining ingredients. Serve immediately.

1 Serving: Calories 370; Total Fat 11g (Saturated Fat 2.5g; Trans Fat 0g); Cholesterol 0mg; Sodium 280mg; Total Carbohydrate 39g (Dietary Fiber 6g); Protein 28g   **Exchanges:** 1 Starch, 1 Other Carbohydrate, 1 Skim Milk, 2½ Very Lean Meat, 1½ Fat   **Carbohydrate Choices:** 2½

mix it up

If you want to be able to sip the whole thing through a straw, skip the garnish, and add all the ingredients to the blender at once.

Store flaxseed meal in the freezer to keep it fresh.

chocolate-banana cookies-and-cream smoothies

PREP TIME: 5 Minutes • **START TO FINISH:** 5 Minutes • 2 servings

1 cup fat-free (skim) milk

4 crème-filled chocolate sandwich cookies

1 pouch (7.6 oz) chocolate-banana-flavor pieces of frozen fruit and yogurt chips smoothie mix

Whipped cream topping in aerosol can, if desired

1 In blender, place milk, cookies and smoothie mix. Cover; blend on high speed 1 minute to 1 minute 30 seconds, stopping to scrape down sides as necessary, until smooth.

2 Pour into 2 glasses. Top each with whipped topping. Serve immediately.

1 Serving: Calories 250; Total Fat 6g (Saturated Fat 1.5g; Trans Fat 0g); Cholesterol 0mg; Sodium 210mg; Total Carbohydrate 40g (Dietary Fiber 2g); Protein 8g   **Exchanges:** 2 Other Carbohydrate, 1 Skim Milk, 1 Fat   **Carbohydrate Choices:** 2½

mix it up

If you like larger pieces of cookie in your smoothies, add the cookies at the end, and pulse a couple of times until the mixture is the desired consistency.

Save a few crumbs from the cookies or crumble up additional cookies to sprinkle over the whipped topping as a garnish.

chocolate-hazelnut breakfast smoothies

PREP TIME: 5 Minutes • **START TO FINISH:** 5 Minutes • 2 servings

1 cup fat-free (skim) milk

½ cup Chocolate Cheerios™ cereal

3 tablespoons hazelnut spread with cocoa

1 pouch (7.6 oz) chocolate-banana-flavor pieces of frozen fruit and yogurt chips smoothie mix

1 In blender, place all ingredients. Cover; blend on high speed 1 minute to 1 minute 30 seconds, stopping to scrape down sides as necessary, until smooth.

2 Pour into 2 glasses. Serve immediately.

1 Serving: Calories 320; Total Fat 10g (Saturated Fat 1g; Trans Fat 0g); Cholesterol 0mg; Sodium 160mg; Total Carbohydrate 49g (Dietary Fiber 4g); Protein 9g **Exchanges:** ½ Starch, 2 Other Carbohydrate, 1 Skim Milk, 1½ Fat **Carbohydrate Choices:** 3

mix it up

Look for hazelnut spread with cocoa in the aisle with the peanut butter.

Substitute Dulce de Leche Cheerios™, Honey Nut Cheerios™ or MultiGrain Cheerios™ for the Chocolate Cheerios if you like.

CALORIE-CONTROLLED DAIRY-FREE

chocolate-raspberry smoothies

PREP TIME: 5 Minutes • **START TO FINISH:** 5 Minutes • 2 servings (1 cup each)

- 2 cups light chocolate soymilk
- 1 cup frozen raspberries
- ½ teaspoon vanilla

1 In blender or food processor, place all ingredients. Cover; blend on low speed about 30 seconds or until smooth.

2 Pour into 2 glasses. Serve immediately.

1 Serving: Calories 130; Total Fat 2g (Saturated Fat 0.5g; Trans Fat 0g); Cholesterol 0mg; Sodium 180mg; Total Carbohydrate 19g (Dietary Fiber 4g); Protein 8g **Exchanges:** ½ Fruit, 1 Skim Milk **Carbohydrate Choices:** 1

peanut butter and berry smoothies

PREP TIME: 5 Minutes • **START TO FINISH:** 5 Minutes • 2 servings (1 cup each)

1 cup light vanilla soymilk

2 tablespoons creamy peanut butter

1 pouch (7.6 oz) strawberry-banana-flavor pieces of frozen fruit and yogurt chips smoothie mix

1 In blender, place all ingredients. Cover; blend on high speed 1 minute to 1 minute 30 seconds, stopping blender to scrape down sides as necessary, until smooth.

2 Pour into 2 glasses. Serve immediately.

1 Serving: Calories 220; Total Fat 11g (Saturated Fat 2g; Trans Fat 0g); Cholesterol 0mg; Sodium 190mg; Total Carbohydrate 23g (Dietary Fiber 3g); Protein 9g   **Exchanges:** ½ Starch, ½ Other Carbohydrate, ½ Low-Fat Milk, ½ High-Fat Meat, 1 Fat   **Carbohydrate Choices:** 1½

mix it up

Plain soymilk can be substituted for vanilla if you would like the smoothies less sweet.

peanut butter–banana smoothies

PREP TIME: 10 Minutes • **START TO FINISH:** 10 Minutes • 4 servings

2 containers (6 oz each) vanilla fat-free yogurt

2 medium bananas, frozen

¼ cup creamy peanut butter

4 teaspoons chopped peanuts

1 In blender, place yogurt, bananas and peanut butter. Cover; blend on high speed until smooth.

2 Pour into 4 glasses. Top each with 1 teaspoon chopped peanuts. Serve immediately.

1 Serving: Calories 230; Total Fat 10g (Saturated Fat 2g; Trans Fat 0g); Cholesterol 0mg; Sodium 120mg; Total Carbohydrate 27g (Dietary Fiber 3g); Protein 8g **Exchanges:** ½ Fruit, 1 Other Carbohydrate, ½ Skim Milk, ½ High-Fat Meat, 1 Fat **Carbohydrate Choices:** 2

mix it up

Peel and slice bananas before freezing so that they are quick and easy to add to smoothies.

cocoa–peanut butter–banana smoothies

PREP TIME: 10 Minutes • **START TO FINISH:** 10 Minutes • 4 servings (1 cup each)

1½ cups creamy vanilla low-fat yogurt (from 2-lb container)

1 cup chocolate milk

¼ cup creamy peanut butter

2 small bananas, sliced

3 to 5 ice cubes

1 cup Cocoa Puffs™ cereal, coarsely crushed*

1 In blender, place yogurt, chocolate milk, peanut butter, bananas and ice cubes. Cover; blend on high speed about 30 seconds or until smooth.

2 Pour into 4 glasses. Sprinkle each with cereal. Serve immediately.

1 Serving: Calories 310; Total Fat 11g (Saturated Fat 3g; Trans Fat 0g); Cholesterol 10mg; Sodium 190mg; Total Carbohydrate 44g (Dietary Fiber 3g); Protein 10g **Exchanges:** 1 Fruit, 1 Other Carbohydrate, 1 Low-Fat Milk, 1½ Fat **Carbohydrate Choices:** 3

* To crush cereal, place in plastic bag or between sheets of waxed paper; crush with rolling pin.

mix it up

Keep a stash of disposable cups with lids so you can breakfast on the go or head outside.

spiced caramel-banana smoothies

PREP TIME: 10 Minutes • **START TO FINISH:** 10 Minutes • 2 servings

1 container (6 oz) crème caramel thick-and-creamy low-fat yogurt

1 ripe medium banana, cut into chunks

1¼ cups soymilk

1 tablespoon caramel fat-free topping

1½ cups crushed ice

¼ teaspoon ground cinnamon

⅛ teaspoon ground cardamom

⅛ teaspoon ground ginger

⅛ teaspoon ground cloves

1 In blender or food processor, place all ingredients. Cover; blend on high speed about 1 minute or until smooth.

2 Pour into 2 glasses. Serve immediately.

1 Serving: Calories 190; Total Fat 2g (Saturated Fat 0g; Trans Fat 0g); Cholesterol 0mg; Sodium 180mg; Total Carbohydrate 36g (Dietary Fiber 2g); Protein 8g **Exchanges:** ½ Fruit, 1 Other Carbohydrate, 1 Skim Milk **Carbohydrate Choices:** 2½

mix it up

If you don't have ground cardamom on hand, you can just increase the amount of cinnamon.

chocolate–peanut butter–banana smoothies

PREP TIME: 5 Minutes • **START TO FINISH:** 5 Minutes • 2 servings (1¼ cups each)

1 large banana, frozen

2 cups light chocolate soymilk

2 tablespoons creamy peanut butter

1 Cut frozen banana into 1-inch chunks. Place banana and remaining ingredients in blender. Cover; blend on high speed about 30 seconds or until smooth.

2 Pour into 2 glasses. Serve immediately.

1 Serving: Calories 260; Total Fat 10g (Saturated Fat 1.5g; Trans Fat 0g); Cholesterol 0mg; Sodium 250mg; Total Carbohydrate 31g (Dietary Fiber 2g); Protein 12g   **Exchanges:** 1½ Fruit, 1 Low-Fat Milk, ½ High-Fat Meat   **Carbohydrate Choices:** 2

mix it up

You can use vanilla soymilk instead of the chocolate for a different flavor.

chocolate-banana protein smoothie shake

PREP TIME: 10 Minutes • **START TO FINISH:** 10 Minutes • 1 serving (1¾ cups)

1 scoop chocolate protein powder (6 tablespoons)

1 cup chocolate-flavored almond milk

1 tablespoon ground flaxseed meal

½ cup frozen chopped banana

1 tablespoon unsweetened baking cocoa

1 In blender, place all ingredients. Cover; blend on high speed until smooth.

2 Pour into large glass. Serve immediately.

1 Serving: Calories 380; Total Fat 8g (Saturated Fat 1.5g; Trans Fat 0g); Cholesterol 0mg; Sodium 240mg; Total Carbohydrate 47g (Dietary Fiber 7g); Protein 28g   **Exchanges:** ½ Fruit, 2 Other Carbohydrate, 1 Skim Milk, 3 Very Lean Meat, 1 Fat   **Carbohydrate Choices:** 3

mix it up

Top this shake with some fat-free whipped topping to add a chocolate-banana cream pie flavor.

You can easily double the ingredients in this shake to make enough to share.

build-me-up peanut butter cup protein smoothie shake

PREP TIME: 10 Minutes • **START TO FINISH:** 10 Minutes • 1 serving (1¾ cups)

1 scoop chocolate protein powder (6 tablespoons)

1 tablespoon unsweetened baking cocoa

1 cup milk

1 tablespoon peanut butter

1 chopped frozen banana

1 tablespoon ground flaxseed meal

1 In blender, place all ingredients. Cover; blend on high speed until smooth.

2 Pour into large glass. Serve immediately.

1 Serving: Calories 510; Total Fat 16g (Saturated Fat 4.5g; Trans Fat 0g); Cholesterol 10mg; Sodium 290mg; Total Carbohydrate 51g (Dietary Fiber 7g); Protein 40g **Exchanges:** 1½ Starch, ½ Fruit, ½ Other Carbohydrate, 1 Skim Milk, 3½ Very Lean Meat, ½ High-Fat Meat, 1½ Fat **Carbohydrate Choices:** 3½

mix it up

For an extra level of decadence, drizzle the top of the shake with chocolate syrup.

Experiment with other nut butters—almond butter is a nice alternative to peanut butter.

Poppers, Pops & Cubes

grab 'n go smoothie poppers

PREP TIME: 5 Minutes • **START TO FINISH:** 2 Hours 5 Minutes • **9 servings (4 poppers each)**

1 medium banana

3 tubes (2.25 oz each) portable yogurt, any flavor (from 1-lb 2-oz box)

1 cup frozen unsweetened whole strawberries

½ cup orange juice

1 In blender, place all ingredients. Cover; blend on high speed about 30 seconds or until smooth.

2 Pour about 1 tablespoon into each of 36 sections of ice cube trays or shaped molds. Freeze at least 2 hours or until firm.

3 Remove smoothie pieces from ice cube trays or molds; place in resealable freezer plastic bag. Store in freezer until ready to use.

1 Serving: Calories 60; Total Fat 1g (Saturated Fat 0g; Trans Fat 0g); Cholesterol 0mg; Sodium 10mg; Total Carbohydrate 11g (Dietary Fiber 1g); Protein 1g **Exchanges:** ½ Starch, ½ Fruit **Carbohydrate Choices:** 1

mix it up

Ice cube trays come in many shapes, so choose a tray that is fun for kids!

Place ice cube trays on a larger tray for ease of moving in and out of the freezer.

fresh fruit frozen yogurt pops

PREP TIME: 10 Minutes • **START TO FINISH:** 6 Hours 10 Minutes • 6 pops

2 containers (6 oz each) French vanilla low-fat yogurt

2 cups cut-up fresh fruit, such as blueberries, bananas, cherries, grapes, papaya, peaches, oranges or raspberries

1 tablespoon honey

6 paper cups (5 oz each) and craft sticks (flat wooden sticks with round ends), or frozen ice pop molds

1 In blender, place yogurt, fruit and honey. Cover; blend until smooth.

2 Divide mixture evenly among paper cups. Cover cups with foil; insert craft stick into center of each pop. (Or fill ice pop molds according to manufacturer's directions.) Freeze about 6 hours or until frozen.

3 To serve, remove foil and peel off paper cups, or remove pops from molds.

1 Pop: Calories 110; Total Fat 1g (Saturated Fat 0g; Trans Fat 0g); Cholesterol 0mg; Sodium 35mg; Total Carbohydrate 22g (Dietary Fiber 1g); Protein 3g   **Exchanges:** 1 Starch, ½ Fruit   **Carbohydrate Choices:** 1½

mix it up

These pops can also be made with strawberries, grapefruit, plums, mango or pineapple.

mango freezer pops

PREP TIME: 15 Minutes • **START TO FINISH:** 11 Hours 15 Minutes • 12 to 16 pops

2 ripe medium mangoes, seeds removed, peeled and cut up

¼ cup sugar

½ cup water

¼ cup fresh lemon juice

3 containers (6 oz each) vanilla fat-free yogurt

12 to 16 paper cups (2 to 4 oz each) and craft sticks (flat wooden sticks with round ends), or frozen ice pop molds

1 In blender, place mangoes, sugar, water and lemon juice. Cover; blend on high speed until smooth. Add yogurt; cover and blend until combined. Pour mixture into 13x9-inch (3-quart) glass baking dish. Cover; freeze about 3 hours, stirring 2 or 3 times, until edges are firm but center is still slightly soft.

2 Scrape mango mixture into chilled large bowl. Beat with electric mixer on medium speed until smooth. Divide mixture evenly among ice pop molds. (If using paper cups, pour mixture into cups. Cover with foil; insert craft stick into center of each pop.) Freeze at least 8 hours or overnight until firm.

3 To serve, remove pops from molds, or remove foil and peel off paper cups.

1 Pop: Calories 80; Total Fat 0g (Saturated Fat 0g; Trans Fat 0g); Cholesterol 0mg; Sodium 20mg; Total Carbohydrate 18g (Dietary Fiber 1g); Protein 1g   **Exchanges:** ½ Starch, ½ Fruit   **Carbohydrate Choices:** 1

mix it up

It's easy to substitute orange juice for the water and the change will only add about 5 calories per serving.

strawberry-peach pops

PREP TIME: 10 Minutes • **START TO FINISH:** 2 Hours 25 Minutes • 10 pops

1 cup fat-free (skim) milk

1 cup frozen unsweetened whole strawberries

⅔ cup creamy peach low-fat yogurt (from 2-lb container)

1 tablespoon sugar, if desired

10 paper cups (3 oz each)

10 craft sticks (flat wooden sticks with round ends)

1 In blender, place milk, strawberries, yogurt and sugar. Cover; blend on high speed about 1 minute or until smooth.

2 Fill each cup with about ¼ cup yogurt mixture. Freeze about 45 minutes or until partially frozen.

3 Insert sticks; freeze about 1 hour 30 minutes longer or until firm.

4 To serve, peel off paper cups.

1 Pop: Calories 50; Total Fat 0.5g (Saturated Fat 0g; Trans Fat 0g); Cholesterol 0mg; Sodium 20mg; Total Carbohydrate 9g (Dietary Fiber 0g); Protein 1g **Exchanges:** ½ Starch **Carbohydrate Choices:** ½

peachy pops

PREP TIME: 10 Minutes • **START TO FINISH:** 2 Hours 10 Minutes • 10 pops

1½ cups vanilla soymilk

2 cups cut-up frozen peaches

⅓ to ½ cup honey

10 paper cups (3 oz each)

10 craft sticks (flat wooden sticks with round ends)

1 In blender, place soymilk, peaches and honey. Cover; blend on high speed about 1 minute or until smooth and frothy.

2 Place paper cups in 13x9-inch pan; divide mixture evenly among paper cups. Freeze 20 to 30 minutes or until partially frozen.

3 Stir each cup with wooden stick; leave stick in center of each cup. Freeze about 1 hour 30 minutes longer or until firm.

4 To serve, peel off paper cups.

1 Pop: Calories 70; Total Fat 0.5g (Saturated Fat 0g; Trans Fat 0g); Cholesterol 0mg; Sodium 25mg; Total Carbohydrate 16g (Dietary Fiber 1g); Protein 1g **Exchanges:** ½ Starch, ½ Other Carbohydrate **Carbohydrate Choices:** 1

strawberry green smoothie pops

PREP TIME: 15 Minutes • **START TO FINISH:** 8 Hours 15 Minutes • 5 pops

1 container (6 oz) French vanilla low-fat yogurt

1 cup sliced fresh strawberries

5 paper cups (5 oz each) and craft sticks (flat wooden sticks with round ends), or frozen ice pop molds

1 container (6 oz) Key lime pie or French vanilla low-fat yogurt

1 cup packed fresh spinach leaves

¼ cup apple juice

1 In blender, place 1 container French vanilla yogurt and the strawberries. Cover; blend until smooth. Spoon 2 tablespoons mixture into each paper cup. Cover cups with foil; insert craft stick into center of each pop. (Or fill ice pop molds according to manufacturer's directions.) Put remaining mixture in bowl; cover and refrigerate. Freeze pops about 2 hours or until frozen.

2 When first layer is frozen, in blender, place Key lime pie yogurt, spinach and apple juice; cover and blend until smooth. Remove foil from pops. Pour about 1½ tablespoons spinach mixture into each cup over frozen layer. Put remaining mixture in bowl; cover and refrigerate. Return foil to pops to support sticks. Freeze about 2 hours longer or until frozen.

3 Repeat with remaining strawberry and spinach layers, freezing at least 2 hours between layers.

4 To serve, remove foil and peel off paper cups, or remove pops from molds.

1 Pop: Calories 90; Total Fat 1g (Saturated Fat 0g; Trans Fat 0g); Cholesterol 0mg; Sodium 45mg; Total Carbohydrate 17g (Dietary Fiber 1g); Protein 3g **Exchanges:** ½ Fruit, ½ Skim Milk **Carbohydrate Choices:** 1

mix it up

For that great layered look, freezing completely between layers is necessary so that colors do not mix into each other.

raspberry lemonade pops

PREP TIME: 15 Minutes • **START TO FINISH:** 8 Hours 15 Minutes • 8 pops

1   can (12 oz) frozen lemonade concentrate

1   cup water

1   cup fresh raspberries

½   cup plain yogurt

10   frozen ice pop molds

10   craft sticks (flat wooden sticks with round ends)

1 In 1-quart saucepan, heat lemonade concentrate and water over medium heat just until lemonade concentrate is completely thawed. Remove from heat; cool.

2 In blender, place ¾ cup of the lemonade mixture, ½ cup of the raspberries and ¼ cup of the yogurt. Cover; blend on medium speed until smooth. Press mixture through small strainer into medium bowl to remove seeds.

3 Divide mixture evenly among ice pop molds. Freeze about 4 hours or until frozen.

4 When first layer is frozen, divide remaining ½ cup raspberries evenly among molds. In small bowl, mix 1 cup lemonade mixture and remaining ¼ cup yogurt. Divide evenly among molds. Cover each mold with foil; insert craft stick into center of each pop. Freeze 4 hours or until frozen.

5 To serve, remove pops from molds.

1 Pop: Calories 110; Total Fat 0.5g (Saturated Fat 0g; Trans Fat 0g); Cholesterol 0mg; Sodium 15mg; Total Carbohydrate 24g (Dietary Fiber 1g); Protein 1g   **Exchanges:** 1½ Other Carbohydrate   **Carbohydrate Choices:** 1½

red, white and blueberry lemonade pops

PREP TIME: 15 Minutes • **START TO FINISH:** 10 Hours 15 Minutes • 6 pops

Red Layer

1 cup sliced fresh strawberries

3 tablespoons lemonade, chilled

1 teaspoon sugar

Equipment

6 paper cups (5 oz each) and craft sticks (flat wooden sticks with round ends), or frozen ice pop molds

White Layer

1 container (6 oz) French vanilla low-fat yogurt

3 tablespoons lemonade, chilled

Blueberry Layer

½ cup fresh blueberries

½ cup lemonade, chilled

½ teaspoon sugar

1 In blender, place red layer ingredients. Cover; blend until smooth. Spoon 2 tablespoons mixture into each paper cup. Cover cups with foil; insert craft stick into center of each pop. (Or fill ice pop molds according to manufacturer's directions.) Freeze about 2 hours or until frozen.

2 When first layer is frozen, in small bowl, mix white layer ingredients until smooth. Remove foil from pops. Spoon about 2 tablespoons mixture into each cup over frozen layer. Return foil to pops to support sticks. Freeze about 2 hours or until frozen.

3 Meanwhile, in blender, place blueberry layer ingredients. Cover; blend until smooth. When white layer is frozen, remove foil from pops. Spoon about 2 tablespoons blueberry mixture into each cup over white layer. Return foil to pops to support sticks. Freeze at least 6 hours or until frozen.

4 To serve, remove foil and peel off paper cups, or remove pops from molds.

1 Pop: Calories 70; Total Fat 0g (Saturated Fat 0g; Trans Fat 0g); Cholesterol 0mg; Sodium 20mg; Total Carbohydrate 14g (Dietary Fiber 1g); Protein 1g **Exchanges:** ½ Starch, ½ Fruit **Carbohydrate Choices:** 1

crazy carrot pops

PREP TIME: 10 Minutes • **START TO FINISH:** 8 Hours 10 Minutes • 6 pops

2 containers (6 oz each) French vanilla low-fat yogurt

2 cups chopped ripe mango

½ cup carrot juice

6 paper cups (5 oz each) and craft sticks (flat wooden sticks with round ends), or frozen ice pop molds

1 cup packed fresh spinach leaves

1 In blender, place yogurt, mango and carrot juice. Cover; blend until smooth. Reserve 1 cup mixture; cover and refrigerate.

2 Divide remaining mixture evenly among paper cups, about ⅓ cup in each. Cover cups with foil; insert craft stick into center of each pop. (Or fill ice pop molds according to manufacturer's directions.) Freeze about 2 hours or until frozen.

3 When first layer is frozen, place reserved mango mixture and spinach in blender. Cover; blend until smooth. Remove foil from pops. Pour about 3 tablespoons spinach mixture into each cup over frozen layer. Return foil to pops to support sticks. Freeze about 6 hours or until frozen.

4 To serve, remove foil and peel off paper cups, or remove pops from molds.

1 Pop: Calories 110; Total Fat 1g (Saturated Fat 0g; Trans Fat 0g); Cholesterol 0mg; Sodium 45mg; Total Carbohydrate 21g (Dietary Fiber 1g); Protein 3g **Exchanges:** 1 Starch, ½ Fruit **Carbohydrate Choices:** 1½

mix it up

To make these pops look like carrots, freeze in 4-ounce paper cone-shaped cups. For sticks, use green straws. To strengthen straws, insert lollipop sticks through straws before freezing.

Look for carrot juice in the refrigerated case of the produce section.

light mai tai tiki pops

PREP TIME: 20 Minutes • **START TO FINISH:** 11 Hours 20 Minutes • 6 pops

Coconut Colada Layer

- 1 container (6 oz) piña colada or Key lime pie fat-free yogurt
- ¼ cup canned coconut milk, well stirred (not cream of coconut)
- 1 teaspoon dark rum

Equipment

- 6 paper cups (5 oz each)
- 6 craft sticks (flat wooden sticks with round ends)

Mango Mai Tai Layer

- 1 ripe mango, peeled, pitted and cubed (about 1 cup)
- 3 tablespoons sugar
- ¾ cup mango nectar, chilled
- 2 tablespoons dark rum
- 2 tablespoons light rum
- 2 tablespoons fresh lime juice
- 1 tablespoon orange-flavor liqueur
- 1 teaspoon amaretto

1 In small bowl, beat coconut colada layer ingredients with whisk until smooth. Divide mixture evenly among paper cups. Cover with foil; insert craft stick into center of each pop. Freeze 2 to 3 hours or until frozen.

2 Meanwhile, in blender, place mango mai tai layer ingredients. Cover; blend on medium speed about 45 seconds, stopping frequently to scrape down sides, until smooth. Cover; refrigerate while waiting for first layer to freeze.

3 When first layer is frozen, remove foil from pops. Pour mango mixture over frozen layer. Return foil to pops to help support sticks. Freeze about 8 hours or until frozen.

4 To serve, remove foil and peel off paper cups.

1 Pop: Calories 130; Total Fat 2g (Saturated Fat 2g; Trans Fat 0g); Cholesterol 0mg; Sodium 20mg; Total Carbohydrate 20g (Dietary Fiber 0g); Protein 1g **Exchanges:** ½ Starch, 1 Other Carbohydrate, ½ Fat **Carbohydrate Choices:** 1

mix it up

Be sure to allow the coconut colada layer to freeze completely before adding the mango mai tai layer.

Be patient when freezing these spiked ice pops. They take longer to freeze because of the alcohol, but they are worth the wait.

watermelon-mojito cocktail pops

PREP TIME: 10 Minutes • **START TO FINISH:** 8 Hours 10 Minutes • 5 pops

2 cups chopped
   seedless watermelon

3 tablespoons sugar

3 tablespoons light rum

3 tablespoons fresh lime juice

3 tablespoons water

4 small fresh mint leaves

5 paper cups (5 oz each)

5 craft sticks (flat wooden
   sticks with round ends)

   Lime slices, if desired

1 In blender, place watermelon, sugar, rum, lime juice, water and mint leaves. Cover; blend until smooth.

2 Divide mixture evenly among paper cups. Cover cups with foil; insert craft stick into center of each pop. Freeze about 8 hours or until frozen.

3 To serve, remove foil; peel off paper cups. Garnish pops with lime slices.

1 Pop: Calories 70; Total Fat 0g (Saturated Fat 0g; Trans Fat 0g); Cholesterol 0mg; Sodium 0mg; Total Carbohydrate 13g (Dietary Fiber 0g); Protein 0g   **Carbohydrate Choices:** 1

mix it up

If you can't find seedless watermelon, make sure to take the seeds out before blending.

coconut-chocolate freezer pops

PREP TIME: 15 Minutes • **START TO FINISH:** 3 Hours 15 Minutes • 11 pops

1 can (14 oz) fat-free sweetened condensed milk (not evaporated)

1 can (14 oz) reduced-fat (lite) coconut milk (not cream of coconut)

¼ teaspoon coconut extract

1 oz bittersweet baking chocolate, shaved

11 paper cups (3 oz each)

11 craft sticks (flat wooden sticks with round ends)

1 In blender, place condensed milk, coconut milk and coconut extract. Cover; blend until well mixed. Stir in chocolate.

2 Divide mixture evenly among paper cups. Cover cups with foil; insert craft stick into center of each pop. Freeze 3 hours or until firm.

3 To serve, remove foil and peel off paper cups.

1 Pop: Calories 140; Total Fat 3.5g (Saturated Fat 3g; Trans Fat 0g); Cholesterol 0mg; Sodium 50mg; Total Carbohydrate 24g (Dietary Fiber 0g); Protein 3g **Exchanges:** 1 Other Carbohydrate, ½ Skim Milk, ½ Fat **Carbohydrate Choices:** 1½

mix it up

If you have frozen ice pop molds, you can use them instead of paper cups. Mold sizes vary, so you may end up with more or fewer pops from this recipe.

fruit smoothie cubes

PREP TIME: 10 Minutes • **START TO FINISH:** 3 Hours 10 Minutes • 24 cubes

3 ripe bananas

1 can (8 oz) crushed pineapple in unsweetened juice, undrained

1 box (10 oz) frozen sliced strawberries in syrup, slightly thawed, broken up

1 Line 24 muffin cups with paper baking cups or use 2 ice cube trays.

2 In blender, place all ingredients. Cover; blend until smooth, stopping to scrape down sides as necessary 2 or 3 times.

3 Divide mixture evenly among muffin cups or 24 sections of ice cube trays, about 2½ tablespoons in each. Freeze 3 hours or until firm.

4 Let fruit cubes stand at room temperature 1 minute. Remove from cups and remove paper, or remove from ice cube trays. Place cubes in resealable freezer plastic bags. Store in freezer until ready to use.

1 Cube: Calories 35; Total Fat 0g (Saturated Fat 0g; Trans Fat 0g); Cholesterol 0mg; Sodium 0mg; Total Carbohydrate 8g (Dietary Fiber 0g); Protein 0g **Exchanges:** ½ Fruit **Carbohydrate Choices:** ½

mix it up

Make these when you have extra bananas on hand or you don't want them to get overripe and go to waste. Then keep these cubes in the freezer for quick smoothies in no time. Blend 3 of the smoothie cubes in the blender with either ¼ cup milk or juice and 1 (6-oz) container of yogurt, or ¾ cup juice.

Bonus

Juice Bar Juicing

If you're new to Juice Bar Juicing, you'll want to know what this craze is all about. So, look here for all the information, tips and tricks you'll need to get started and become a pro at making juices.

Juice bars have been popping up all over the country. Why the buzz? Juicing is an easy way to incorporate more fresh produce into anyone's diet. And a diet that's rich in produce can make you feel fabulous. But if you frequent juicing shops, you'll find that menu items can be pricy and that is a good reason to start making your own juices. But also, you may decide that you like blending your own flavors. You'll want to be aware of calorie and sugar content from the concentrated mixtures that you get when the bulk and most of the fiber is removed from the fruits and vegetables. So the idea is that juices should not replace fruits and veggies in your diet but rather should complement the nutrients you're already eating.

choosing a juicer

There are many brands of juicers on the market, and like any kitchen gadget, it's hard to know which one to pick or how much money to invest in one that will suit your lifestyle. Many consumers new to the juicing scene opt to buy a less expensive version and work their way up to a more professional setup as juicing becomes a part of their routine. Then again, if the juicer you purchase isn't high quality, or isn't convenient to use or clean, you might become discouraged from getting into the habit of juicing to begin with.

First, research the types of juicer that will suit your needs and budget, then read reviews and ask friends or the staff at your local juice/smoothie bar for recommendations. There are two different types of juicers to choose from: slow juicers and

centrifugal juicers. Each has its unique features—which may be either pros or cons to you—depending on your preferences.

Slow juicers Also known as upright juicers, slow juicers use a single auger to crush and squeeze the produce to extract juice from it. Don't be fooled by the name—this kind of juicer takes just a few minutes longer than the other type of juicer to make juice. Less heat and air are generated during the juicing process with this type of juicer, which helps retain nutrients, provide a prettier colored juice that holds its color well and produces a juice with less foam.

With a slow juicer, the juice will be somewhat thicker in texture because more fiber is retained with the juice as it is processed. If you want to process nuts, such as almonds to make almond milk, this is the only machine that can do the job. Plus, this type of juicer also works well with all leafy greens. If you are looking for a juicer that tends to be smaller, is louder when used but blade free and offers easy cleanup, this is a good choice.

Centrifugal juicers Also known as a high-speed juicer, this type of juicer separates the juice from the pulp with high-speed spinning of the produce. Be ready for these machines to work through large quantities of produce very quickly with their wide feeding tubes and fast juicing process. This leads to little or no prep since the produce doesn't need to be cut as small to fit through the feeding tubes—or at all.

This style of juicer is great for making juice in larger quantities (for those juicing for a family or making enough juice to have some on hand), and the juice has less pulp (for those who tend to lean toward drinking juice that's "pulp free"). Juices from this style juicer can produce more foam or juice that comes out in layers and is harder to stir to an even color and consistency. The oxidation that happens with this style of juicer can cause the juice to change color more quickly as well, as it is exposed to the air. Some high-speed juicers come with (or can be purchased as accessories) disks that are made specifically to process soft or hard foods. Most of the removable parts from these juicers can be cleaned in the dishwasher, but the blades are sharp, so care is needed when handling them.

stocking up

Once you're juicing regularly, you'll want to keep plenty of fresh produce on hand. Most important, choose vibrant, *fresh* produce—not produce that is past its prime. Juices will only be as good as the produce that you make them with.

prepping your produce

- Wash produce thoroughly before cutting. You'll need to cut produce just small enough to fit through the feeding tube of your juicer. Most fruits and veggies can be juiced with the skin, stems and leaves intact. Leaves like lettuce or kale are best juiced when rolled up tightly into balls before adding to the juicer. (If you try adding them flat, they may just stay in the juicer without getting juiced or broken down in any way.)

- Make sure to remove stone-fruit pits, pineapple and melon rinds and citrus peel and pith (the bitter-tasting white part beneath the peel).

- To peel or not to peel? That is the question! For produce like carrots that grows in the ground or for produce that may be chemically treated for pests, you need to decide whether you are

can a blender be used for juicing?

Ask this question and you might just find yourself in the middle of a heated debate! Technically, juicers separate the juice from the fiber (or most of it) and blenders just finely chop the fiber with the juice—so making juice in a blender is actually more like a smoothie. Leaving the fiber in the juice isn't necessarily a bad thing—the juice will have more texture (which some may like and some may not), and when you drink the fiber with the juice, it can help you feel fuller longer. However, unless your blender is a super-heavy-duty professional model (also known as

a whole food juicer), it probably isn't strong enough to blend hard produce.

Most blenders might work for softer produce if you peel and chop it first. You may need to add ice cubes or liquid, such as juice or water, to help it blend properly, and you may need to stop and turn off the blender to press the produce closer to the blades in order for it to chop evenly. If you want to use your blender to make juice and like your juice "pulp free," you could try to strain it using a fine-mesh strainer or cheesecloth.

comfortable with how clean they are when scrubbed or whether you should peel them before juicing. If you prefer, leave the skin on fruits like apples and pears—they can be easily washed first and the peel can add to the color and boost the nutrient makeup of the juice since some nutrients are concentrated in the skins.

- Herbs with stems can be added by wrapping the stems (with the leaves) around other pieces of produce being juiced so that they will be processed as well and not left stuck inside the juicer unprocessed.

- Alternate adding different produce pieces, in small batches, to your juicer. That way, things that aren't as juicy and may have a harder time being processed by the juicer can be followed up with pieces that are juicier and can "push them through." Allow what you added to be almost completely processed before you add another batch. If you add something and it seems stuck in the juicer, add a tablespoon or two of the juice that has already been processed to help it move through the juicer.

start slowly

- Since it's going straight from the fruit or vegetable to your glass—without any other processing, pasteurizing or storage—fresh juice can taste quite a bit different from, and more intense than, what comes out of an orange juice carton. Before you purchase anything in bulk, experiment by making different juices on your own or tasting them at a local made-to-order juice bar to see what combinations you like.

- If you're new to drinking juices, start with more heavily fruit-based juices. As you decide you like more vegetables (in terms of taste and digestibility), slowly change to juices that are more vegetable-heavy and have less fruit.

- For the best flavor, a little fruit added with the veggies can make the juice taste a whole lot better! Apples or pears play great supporting roles in vegetable juices. Experiment with the varieties (some are sweeter than others) to see which ones you like with your veggies. Does your new creation taste a bit ho-hum? Perk up the flavor or cut through the earthiness of kale, beets or spinach with lemon or lime, or add just a hint of other flavorful ingredients, such as gingerroot or fresh herbs, to excite your taste buds.

- Eye appeal is another aspect of juicing to keep in mind. A beautiful-colored juice will be a lot easier to drink than one that looks like it came from the bottom of a pond! Think about what colors of produce you are adding, and take note as you try different combinations. You'll discover what you like and which ones make juice that doesn't look as appetizing to drink. Just a tweak from a red apple to a green-skinned one or from green cabbage to purple cabbage may be all you need to turn out a juice that's really pretty to look at as well as tasty to drink! See our recipes for inspiration. They boast a variety of colors and flavors to get you started.

mix and match

There are no hard-and-fast rules for juice, but flavor profiles and water-ratio balance are important to keep in mind. For example, a juice made from celery and cucumber may be watery tasting and produce a large amount of juice, whereas a juice made entirely of root vegetables like carrots and beets may be very rich and produce a small amount of juice.

pick one or two to use as a base:

- Carrot
- Celery
- Cucumber
- Orange
- Grapefruit
- Melon
- Pineapple

pick one or two (use a medium amount, to taste):

- Bell pepper
- Beet
- Apple
- Grapes
- Berries
- Kiwifruit
- Spinach, kale or other greens
- Pear
- Peach

optional "accent" flavors (use a tiny to small amount, to taste)

- Parsley
- Watercress
- Gingerroot
- Garlic
- Mint
- Lemon
- Lime

starting combos (use these as a jumping-off place for your own concoctions):

fruity

- Carrot + apple +ginger
- Grapefruit + orange + kiwifruit
- Pineapple + peach + ginger
- Watermelon + cucumber + lime + mint

veggie

- Cucumber + beet + parsley
- Celery + kale + green grapes
- Carrot + beet + spinach
- Carrot + bell pepper + watercress

pulp for what purpose?

You will find that when you juice, pulp happens—a lot of it. What do you do with all that pulp?

Some people suggest saving all the pulp in a resealable food-storage freezer bag in the freezer and adding it to meat loaves, quick breads, and the like. But if you left stems, seeds, etc. on your produce when you juiced it, you may not wish to add it to things you will eat. That pulp is a great addition to a composting bin, if you have one. If you don't have a compost bin, find a neighbor who does—they'll be excited to get your "gifts"! A slick trick to keep the pulp basket clean (for a slow juicer) is to line it with one of the thin plastic produce bags you get from the grocery store.

spicy orange sunrise

PREP TIME: 10 Minutes • **START TO FINISH:** 10 Minutes • 2 servings (about ¾ cup each)

3 medium carrots (8 inch; about 8 oz total)

1 medium mango (about 1 lb), pit removed

1 jumbo orange (3¼ inches in diameter; about 11 oz), peeled

1 piece (1 inch) gingerroot

1 Turn juicer on. Alternate adding ingredients, a little at a time, to juicer until fruit and vegetables are processed into juice.

2 Stir juice well; pour into 2 glasses. Serve immediately. Discard pulp.

1 Serving: Calories 210; Total Fat 1g (Saturated Fat 0g; Trans Fat 0g); Cholesterol 0mg; Sodium 75mg; Total Carbohydrate 47g (Dietary Fiber 8g); Protein 3g **Exchanges:** 3 Fruit, 1 Vegetable **Carbohydrate Choices:** 3

mix it up

Wrap any remaining gingerroot tightly in plastic wrap and place in a small resealable freezer plastic bag. Store it in the freezer for the next time you want to make juice or smoothies. It will keep for 2 to 3 months.

raspberry-lime juice

PREP TIME: 10 Minutes • **START TO FINISH:** 10 Minutes • 2 servings (about ¾ cup each)

2 sweet red-skinned apples (about 8 oz each)

1 package (6 oz) fresh raspberries (1⅓ cups)

½ medium lime, peeled

1 Turn juicer on. Alternate adding ingredients, a little at a time, to juicer until fruit is processed into juice.

2 Stir juice well; pour into 2 glasses. Serve immediately. Discard pulp.

1 Serving: Calories 170; Total Fat 1g (Saturated Fat 0g; Trans Fat 0g); Cholesterol 0mg; Sodium 0mg; Total Carbohydrate 40g (Dietary Fiber 10g); Protein 1g **Exchanges:** 2½ Fruit **Carbohydrate Choices:** 2½

mix it up

For a twist with beets, alternate adding ½ medium (3-inch) beet with the other ingredients. (If necessary, add 1 to 2 tablespoons of the juice mixture already processed to help push the remaining juice from the beet out of the machine.)

Sweet varieties of apples that work well in this juice include Regent, Gala and Fuji. Leave the skin on so it can add to the red color of the juice.

purple juice pick-me-up

PREP TIME: 10 Minutes • **START TO FINISH:** 10 Minutes • 2 servings (about ¾ cup each)

¼ head red cabbage, core removed (8 oz)

2 small red-skinned apples (about 4 oz each)

½ medium lemon, peeled

1 cup seedless black grapes (about 6 oz)

6 large fresh basil leaves

1 Turn juicer on. Alternate adding ingredients, a little at a time, to juicer (wrap basil leaves around pieces of apple before juicing) until fruit and vegetables are processed into juice.

2 Stir juice well; pour into 2 glasses. Serve immediately. Discard pulp.

1 Serving: Calories 170; Total Fat 0.5g (Saturated Fat 0g; Trans Fat 0g); Cholesterol 0mg; Sodium 35mg; Total Carbohydrate 38g (Dietary Fiber 6g); Protein 2g **Exchanges:** 2 Fruit, 2 Vegetable **Carbohydrate Choices:** 2½

mix it up

Leave the peel on the apples when juicing them. The red skin adds to the lovely color of the juice.

soothing spa sipper

PREP TIME: 10 Minutes • **START TO FINISH:** 10 Minutes • 2 servings (about 1 cup each)

1   cucumber (8 inch; 12 oz)

¼   honeydew melon, rind removed (about 8 oz)

¼   fresh pineapple, rind removed, cored (8 oz)

1   large stem fresh mint with leaves (about 10 leaves)

1 Turn juicer on. Alternate adding ingredients, a little at a time, to juicer (wrap stem of mint leaves around piece of cucumber before juicing) until fruit and vegetables are processed into juice.

2 Stir juice well; pour into 2 glasses. Serve immediately. Discard pulp.

1 Serving: Calories 140; Total Fat 0g (Saturated Fat 0g; Trans Fat 0g); Cholesterol 0mg; Sodium 25mg; Total Carbohydrate 31g (Dietary Fiber 4g); Protein 2g   **Exchanges:** 2 Fruit, 1 Vegetable   **Carbohydrate Choices:** 2

mix it up

Stir this juice into some cold sparkling water for a refreshing beverage that you can sip a little longer.

refreshing green juice

PREP TIME: 10 Minutes • **START TO FINISH:** 10 Minutes • 2 servings (about 1⅓ cups each)

8 large leaves fresh green kale, ½ inch of stem ends cut off (6 oz)

1 medium Bartlett pear (9 oz)

¼ bunch fresh cilantro (1 oz)

½ medium lemon, peeled

1 Turn juicer on. Alternate adding ingredients, a little at a time, to juicer until fruit and vegetables are processed into juice.

2 Stir juice well; pour into 2 glasses. Serve immediately. Discard pulp.

1 Serving: Calories 140; Total Fat 1g (Saturated Fat 0g; Trans Fat 0g); Cholesterol 0mg; Sodium 45mg; Total Carbohydrate 29g (Dietary Fiber 6g); Protein 3g   **Exchanges:** 1½ Fruit, 1½ Vegetable **Carbohydrate Choices:** 2

mix it up

This is a great way to get nutrient-packed kale into your diet. When it's surrounded with the yumminess of pear and cilantro, you won't even taste it!

metric conversion guide

Note: The recipes in this cookbook have not been developed or tested using metric measures.
When converting recipes to metric, some variations in quality may be noted.

Volume

U.S. Units	Canadian Metric	Australian Metric
¼ teaspoon	1 mL	1 ml
½ teaspoon	2 mL	2 ml
1 teaspoon	5 mL	5 ml
1 tablespoon	15 mL	20 ml
¼ cup	50 mL	60 ml
⅓ cup	75 mL	80 ml
½ cup	125 mL	125 ml
⅔ cup	150 mL	170 ml
¾ cup	175 mL	190 ml
1 cup	250 mL	250 ml
1 quart	1 liter	1 liter
1½ quarts	1.5 liters	1.5 liters
2 quarts	2 liters	2 liters
2½ quarts	2.5 liters	2.5 liters
3 quarts	3 liters	3 liters
4 quarts	4 liters	4 liters

Weight

U.S. Units	Canadian Metric	Australian Metric
1 ounce	30 grams	30 grams
2 ounces	55 grams	60 grams
3 ounces	85 grams	90 grams
4 ounces (¼ pound)	115 grams	125 grams
8 ounces (½ pound)	225 grams	225 grams
16 ounces (1 pound)	455 grams	500 grams
1 pound	455 grams	0.5 kilogram

Measurements

Inches	Centimeters
1	2.5
2	5.0
3	7.5
4	10.0
5	12.5
6	15.0
7	17.5
8	20.5
9	23.0
10	25.5
11	28.0
12	30.5
13	33.0

Temperatures

Fahrenheit	Celsius
32°	0°
212°	100°
250°	120°
275°	140°
300°	150°
325°	160°
350°	180°
375°	190°
400°	200°
425°	220°
450°	230°
475°	240°
500°	260°

index

Page numbers in *italics* indicate illustrations

Recipe Testing and Calculating Nutrition Information

Recipe Testing:

- Large eggs and 2% milk were used unless otherwise indicated.

- Fat-free, low-fat, low-sodium or lite products were not used unless indicated.

- No nonstick cookware and bakeware were used unless otherwise indicated. No dark-colored, black or insulated bakeware was used.

- When a pan is specified, a metal pan was used; a baking dish or pie plate means ovenproof glass was used.

- An electric hand mixer was used for mixing only when mixer speeds are specified.

Calculating Nutrition:

- The first ingredient was used wherever a choice is given, such as ⅓ cup sour cream or plain yogurt.

- The first amount was used wherever a range is given, such as 3- to 3½-pound whole chicken.

- The first serving number was used wherever a range is given, such as 4 to 6 servings.

- "If desired" ingredients were not included.

- Only the amount of a marinade or frying oil that is absorbed was included.